EXPLORE
FOSSILS!

Cynthia Light Brown & Grace Brown

Illustrated by Bryan Stone

Recent titles in the **Explore Your World!** Series

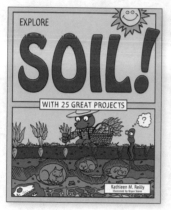

Check out more titles at www.nomadpress.net

Nomad Press
A division of Nomad Communications
10 9 8 7 6 5 4 3 2 1

This book was manufactured by Marquis Book Printing,
Montmagny, Québec, Canada
January 2016, Job #120819

ISBN Softcover: 978-1-61930-335-5
ISBN Hardcover: 978-1-61930-331-7

Illustrations by Bryan Stone
Educational Consultant, Marla Conn

Questions regarding the ordering of this book should be addressed to
Nomad Press
2456 Christian St.
White River Junction, VT 05001
www.nomadpress.net
Printed in Canada.

CONTENTS

Interested in primary sources? Look for this icon.

Use a smartphone or tablet app to scan the QR code and explore more!
You can find a list of URLs on the Resources page.

If the QR code doesn't work, try searching the Internet with
the Keyword Prompts to find other helpful sources.

KEYWORD PROMPTS

fossil discoveries   🔍

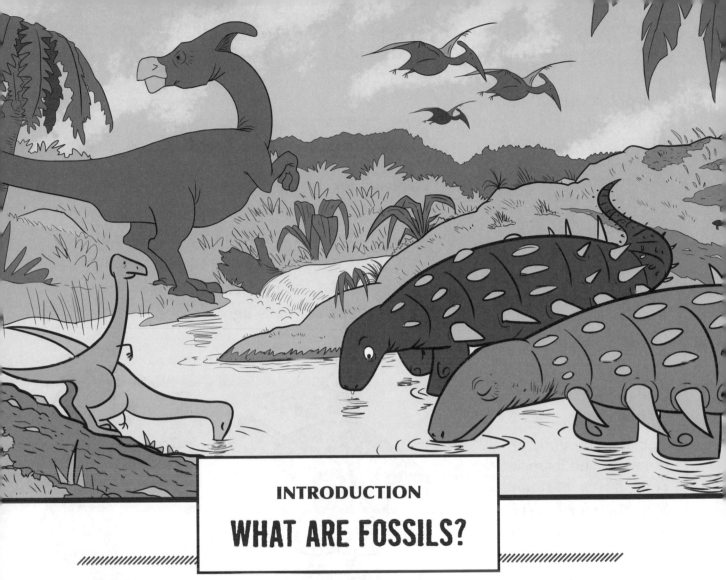

INTRODUCTION

WHAT ARE FOSSILS?

Millions of years ago, huge animals roamed the earth. Some weighed more than 10 times as much as an elephant. Have you heard of these creatures? They're dinosaurs! But if dinosaurs lived so long ago, how do we know so much about them?

The answer can be found in what they left behind. A fossil is the remains of an ancient plant or animal that has been preserved in rock. Have you ever found a strange-looking rock that looked like a seashell or had an imprint of a leaf or an animal track? It was probably a fossil.

WORDS TO KNOW

fossil: the remains of any organism, including animals and plants, that have been preserved in rock.

1

WORDS TO KNOW

paleontology: the study of the fossils of plants and animals. A scientist who studies paleontology is a paleontologist.

environment: everything in nature, living and nonliving, including plants, animals, soil, rocks, and water.

archaeology: the study of ancient people through the objects they left behind. A scientist who studies archaeology is a archaeologist.

geology: the study of the earth and its rocks. A scientist who studies geology is a geologist.

biology: the study of living things.

organism: any living thing.

WHAT IS PALEONTOLOGY?

Paleontology is the study of ancient life. Scientists called paleontologists study fossils to find out about plants and animals that lived long ago. Paleontologists want to know what the earth's environment was like millions of years ago.

Archaeology is the study of human remains and objects made by humans. Paleontology includes the study of all life, from ferns to dinosaurs to elephants. Paleontologists and archaeologists sometimes work together. For example, a paleontologist might help identify plant fossils at an archaeological site. This can help determine what the early humans who lived there ate.

Paleontology combines geology and biology. A paleontologist must understand organisms, as well as how rocks form and move on the surface of the earth.

GOOD SCIENCE PRACTICES

Every good scientist keeps a science journal! Choose a notebook to use as your science journal. As you read through this book and do the activities, keep track of your observations in a scientific method worksheet, like the one shown here. Scientists use the scientific method to keep their experiments organized.

Step	Example
1. Question: What are we trying to find out? What problem are we trying to solve?	Did dinosaurs live in your sandbox?
2. Research: What do other people think?	Books and articles show that other people have found dinosaur fossils in your town.
3. Hypothesis/Prediction: What do we think the answer will be?	I think dinosaurs lived in my sandbox.
4. Equipment: What supplies are we using?	Walking shoes, small shovel, magnifying glass, science journal
5. Method: What procedure are we following?	Divide sandbox into sections and dig carefully. Examine rocks for fossils.
6. Results: What happened and why?	Did you find any dinosaur fossils? If so, dinosaurs might have lived in your sandbox!

Each chapter of this book begins with a question to help guide your exploration of fossils. Keep the question in your mind as you read the chapter. At the end of each chapter, use your science journal to record your thoughts and answers.

? **INVESTIGATE!**

Why do we use geologic time when we talk about the history of the earth? Why not use human time?

geologic timescale: the way the 4.6-billion-year history of the earth is divided up.

WORDS TO KNOW

TIMELINE OF THE EARTH

Can you imagine living through a day that isn't divided into hours? How would you know when to eat lunch or when to go to bed? People divide time into different units to help us keep track of time. These units include years, months, weeks, days, hours, minutes, and seconds.

Geologists divide the entire history of the earth into units, too. They call this history the *geologic timescale*. The parts of the geologic timescale are based on when different kinds of life developed and on other events in the earth's history.

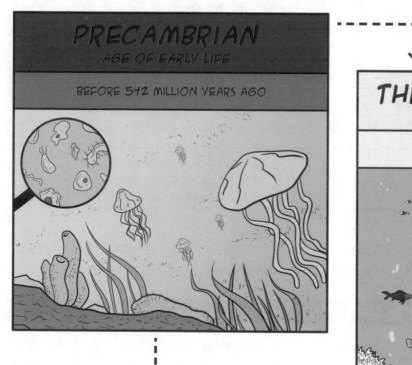

PRECAMBRIAN
AGE OF EARLY LIFE

BEFORE 542 MILLION YEARS AGO

THE PALEOZOIC ERA
AGE OF FISHES

542 TO 252 MILLION YEARS AGO

It's a bit like if you divided your own life into units such as babyhood, preschool, and elementary school. The different periods in your life aren't all the same length. The different periods in the geologic timescale are all different, too.

The word *fossil* comes from the Latin word *fossilis*, which means "dug up."

The earth has been around for more than 4 billion years. That's a lot of time to divide! There are four large periods of time.

✳ Precambrian is before 542 million years ago.

✳ Paleozoic Era is between 542 and 252 million years ago.

✳ Mesozoic Era is between 252 and 65 million years ago.

✳ Cenozoic Era is between now and 65 million years ago.

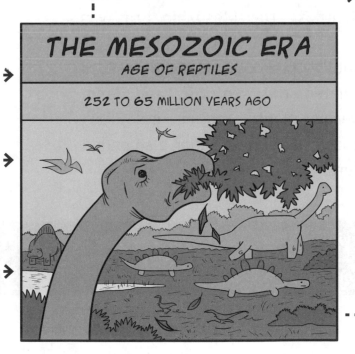

THE MESOZOIC ERA
AGE OF REPTILES

252 TO 65 MILLION YEARS AGO

THE CENOZOIC ERA
AGE OF MAMMALS

65 MILLION YEARS TO TODAY

microorganism: an organism that is so small it can only be seen with a microscope.

reptile: an animal usually covered with scales that lays eggs in dry places. Reptiles include snakes, lizards, turtles, and now-extinct dinosaurs.

extinction: the disappearance of a species from the earth.

species: a group of living things that are closely related and can produce young.

pterosaur: an extinct flying reptile with featherless wings of the Mesozoic Period.

mammal: a type of animal, such as a human, dog, or cat. Mammals are usually born live, feed milk to their young, and usually have hair or fur covering most of their skin.

mass extinction: periods in the earth's history when very large numbers of species die out in a short period of time.

PRECAMBRIAN: Sometimes called the "Age of Early Life," Precambrian was the time before 542 million years ago. The seas contained mats of algae, microorganisms, and simple animals, such as sponges and jellyfish.

THE PALEOZOIC ERA: Sometimes called the "Age of Fishes," the Paleozoic Era was between 542 and 252 million years ago. There were lots of fish, corals, and other ocean creatures. Ferns, evergreen forests, insects, and reptiles lived on land. The Paleozoic Era ended with the largest extinction of species in the history of the earth.

THE MESOZOIC ERA: Called the "Age of Reptiles," the Mesozoic Era was between 252 and 65 million years ago. Crocodiles, pterosaurs, and dinosaurs dominated the sea, air, and land. Flowering plants and mammals first appeared. A mass extinction also ended this era.

PS

The National Park Service celebrates National Fossil Day during Earth Science Week in October each year. You can join the celebration. **Check it out on this website.**

KEYWORD PROMPTS

national fossil day

THE CENOZOIC ERA: Called the "Age of Mammals," the Cenozoic Era is between now and 65 million years ago. Birds and mammals grew in importance. Horses, mammoths, and humans appeared during the Cenozoic Era.

These big blocks of time are broken down into smaller units. You might have heard of one of the smaller units, the Jurassic Period. The Jurassic is one of three periods during the Mesozoic Era.

The book and movie *Jurassic Park* is named after the Jurassic Period because dinosaurs lived then.

Fossils are like pieces of a puzzle that can tell us about the history of the earth. Right where you're standing, dinosaurs might have roamed or coral reefs might have grown. Maybe an early human ancestor once stood in the same spot! Fossils give us clues about what the earth was like millions of years ago.

In *Explore Fossils!*, you'll learn about different types of fossils and how they form. You'll also learn about how paleontologists use clues found in fossils to show how life on the earth has changed through time. You'll make a plaster fossil and learn how to hunt for your own fossils. Maybe you'll discover a new plant or creature that no one has ever heard of before!

? INVESTIGATE!

It's time to consider and discuss:
Why do we use geologic time when we talk about the history of the earth? Why not use human time?

TAKE A WALK THROUGH TIME

Life began on the earth a very long time ago. Compared with when life first appeared, humans have been around for a very, very short period of time. This activity will help you think about geologic time compared to human time.

1 Ask a friend or an adult to help you. Find a place where you can walk safely for 10 minutes or so without stopping, such as a walking path or your school playground. Start walking and count out loud together for every step you take.

2 When you get to the steps listed in the chart, say the step first, then what happened. Then keep walking and counting. Each step you take represents 10 million years.

THINGS TO NOTICE: Whew! That was a lot of walking! Humans only came into the picture at the very, very end of your walk. What does this tell you about our place in geologic time?

  (PS) Many of the names in this book are hard to say, but you can hear them spoken online. **Go to Merriam-Webster.com, search for the word, and press the ◀) symbol next to your word to hear it spoken.**

→ **KEYWORD PROMPTS**

merriam-webster 🔍

Precambrian	**Step 1:** 4 billion, 600 million years ago.	Earth formed
	Step 110: Stromatolites from cyanobacteria probably appeared about 3 billion 500 million years ago.	Oldest fossils
	Step 250: Cells with nuclei appeared about 2 billion 100 million years ago, possibly earlier.	First cells with a nucleus
	Step 390: Simple sponges appeared about 600 million years ago.	First sponges
Paleozoic	**Step 405:** The earth teemed with life starting about 542 million years ago.	First abundant life
	Step 407: Early jawless fish appeared 530 million years ago.	First fish
	Step 435: A major extinction kills up to 96 percent of life about 250 million years ago.	The Great Dying
Mesozoic	**Step 436:** Dinosaurs first appeared almost 225 million years ago.	First dinosaurs
	Step 438: Mammals first appeared about 220 million years ago.	First mammals
	Step 453: Dinosaurs became extinct 65 million years ago.	Dinosaurs extinct
Cenozoic	**Step 458:** Horses appeared about 23 million years ago.	First horses
	Step 459½: Human ancestors appeared about 5.5 million years ago.	First human ancestors
	Step 459¾: Humans appeared almost 3 million years ago.	First humans
	Step 459$^{999}/_{1000}$: Ancient Egyptians build the pyramids 4,645 years ago.	First Pyramids
	Step 460	Present day

CHAPTER 1

FROM THE ROCKS

Fossils tell the story of ancient life. But it's not easy to go from being a living organism to being a fossil. It's a complicated process that can take millions of years!

Fossils come in different shapes and sizes. They are divided into three types:

* body fossils
* trace fossils
* chemical fossils

? INVESTIGATE!

What can fossils tell us about the kinds of environments that existed long ago?

BODY FOSSILS are made from the bodies of organisms. This kind of fossil includes the hard parts of animals, such as bones, teeth, and shells. Petrified wood, seeds, and seed casings are other examples of body fossils. An entire organism trapped in amber is a body fossil.

TRACE FOSSILS are formed when an organism acts on its environment. You can think of it as fossilized behavior. Foot or paw prints, claw marks, and marks from a tail dragging in sand or mud are all trace fossils. Nests, eggs, burrows, holes, and spaces left by roots of plants are more examples.

Even poop can turn into a fossil! Fossilized poop that turned to stone long ago is called coprolite. Another group of trace fossils are called gastroliths. These are stones found in the stomachs of some animals. The stones help digest food.

petrified wood: a fossil of wood that has been turned to stone.

amber: hard, fossilized resin. Resin is a sticky substance that oozes from trees.

WORDS TO KNOW

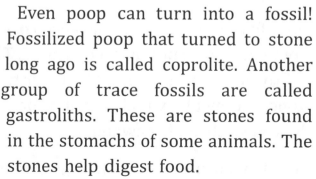

WHAT DO YOU CALL A PALEONTOLOGIST WHO NEVER GETS ANY WORK DONE?

HA HA HA

Lazy bones!

carbon: an element found in living things, including plants. Carbon is also found in diamonds, charcoal, and graphite.

sedimentary rocks: rocks formed from sediments or the remains of plants or animals. Sedimentary rock can also form from the evaporation of seawater.

sediments: small particles of rocks or minerals, such as clay, sand, or pebbles.

evaporation: when a liquid heats up and changes to a gas.

erosion: the gradual wearing away of rock or soil by water and wind.

CHEMICAL FOSSILS are chemicals found in rocks that were made by living creatures long ago. They include natural gas and oil. Some of the oldest evidence of life comes from a certain type of carbon that was produced by microorganisms nearly 3.5 billion years ago.

SEDIMENTARY ROCKS

Most fossils form in sedimentary rocks. These are rocks made from sediments such as sand or mud. The sediments are pressed tightly and often cemented together to form stone. Sedimentary rock can also form from the evaporation of seawater.

Rain, wind, and ice break larger rocks into smaller and smaller pieces. This is a process called weathering, or erosion.

Water or air carries the sediments to other places while breaking them into even smaller pieces. As more sediments land in one area, they get buried deeper and pressed together. Heat and pressure change the soft sediments into hard sedimentary rocks.

WHERE DID THE PALEONTOLOGIST FIND THE BONES?

In a foss-hill!

Sedimentary rocks can have layers of different kinds of rock, one on top of the other. When they first form, the layers are horizontal. Once they become rocks, the layers can tilt or fold because of forces in the earth.

Different sedimentary rocks form in different environments. A river might carry small and large sizes of sediments. The ocean floor usually contains tiny sediments, or mud. Sedimentary rocks are forming all of the time, even right now!

HOW A FOSSIL FORMS

Most plants and animals never become fossils. They decay first. Lots of steps have to happen for an organism to become a fossil.

WORDS TO KNOW

decay: to rot.

13

minerals: solids that are found in rocks and in the ground. Rocks are made of minerals. Gold and diamonds are precious minerals.

When a plant or animal dies, the remains usually break apart or are eaten by other creatures. But sometimes they are buried quickly by sediments such as sand or mud. Then they have the chance to become fossils.

The soft tissue, including the skin, usually rots away. Water with minerals dissolved in it seeps into the sediments and fills the tiny pores in the bones and shells. In rare cases, even the soft parts of a plant or animal, such as skin and organs, are replaced by minerals.

More sediments pile on. The pressure and heat from the weight of all of those sediments harden the mineral solution and the surrounding sediments into rock. A fossil is born!

Much later, the rock might be lifted up by movements in the earth. If the rocks above the fossil are eroded by wind, water, and ice, it leaves the fossil exposed to be found by us.

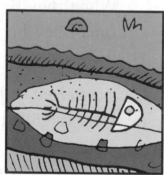

Footprints and other trace fossils are formed when an organism makes a mark in sand or mud. The mark is covered and filled in by sediment, which then hardens into a fossil.

BRUSH BRUSH

EARLY FOSSIL HUNTERS

People have been interested in fossils for a long time. But they didn't always understand what fossils were or where they came from.

Long ago, people thought fossils came from the sky or grew from the earth. The ancient Chinese thought that large fossilized dinosaur bones came from flying dragons. In the Middle Ages, Europeans thought fossils were the remains of Noah's flood. Maybe giant bones came from giant humans.

In the 1600s, a Danish physician and priest named Nicolas Steno studied fossils. He was one of the first people to prove that fossils are the remains of once-living organisms. Steno compared tongue-shaped stones with the teeth of living sharks. He showed that they were teeth from ancient sharks.

THE FATHER OF PALEONTOLOGY

Georges Cuvier is sometimes called the "Father of Paleontology." He showed that rock layers in one area could be matched to rocks in other areas based on the fossils contained in the rocks. Cuvier proved that animals can become extinct. This was a crazy idea at the time! He compared the remains of elephants to fossils of mammoths to show they weren't the same species.

 You can compare the remains too. What is different about these two jawbones?

KEYWORD PROMPTS

Cuvier mammoth jaw 🔍

WORDS TO KNOW

evolve: to change over time, sometimes into something more complex.

theory of evolution: a scientific theory that explains how species change over time.

Richard Owen described the fossil *Archaeopteryx* in 1863. It had wings like a bird and teeth like a dinosaur. *Archaeopteryx* was shown to be a bridge between dinosaurs and birds.

Paleontologist Charles Lyell showed that there was a sequence of fossils through time. Charles Darwin combined Lyell's observations with his own of the natural world. He suggested that new species evolve over time. In 1859, Darwin published *On the Origin of Species*, which explained the theory of evolution.

Scientists have taken the understanding developed by these early scientists and expanded it. Now, we have a good understanding of the development of life on earth through time from fossils.

? INVESTIGATE!

It's time to consider and discuss: What can fossils tell us about the kinds of environments that existed long ago?

SOAP EROSION

Rocks are eroded by wind, water, and ice. Try this activity to get an idea of one way a rock can erode.

SUPPLIES

* bar of soap
* sponge slightly larger than the soap
* kitchen or bathroom sink

1 Place the bar of soap on top of the sponge. Set the sponge under the faucet of the kitchen or bathroom sink. Let the rest of your family know what you're doing so they won't disturb your experiment!

2 Start a scientific method worksheet in your study journal. What do you think will happen to the soap after sitting under dripping water for 5 minutes? An hour? Two hours?

3 Turn the faucet on so that it slowly drips water onto the soap.

4 Check back after a few minutes and again after about an hour. Does the soap look different? If not, keep the soap under the dripping faucet longer.

THINGS TO NOTICE: How has the dripping water changed the appearance of the soap? Would it take the water a shorter or longer amount of time to erode rock compared with soap? Why? What would happen if you increased or decreased how fast the water drips? Try it out and see if your predictions are correct.

SUPPLIES

* clear plastic cup
* M&Ms, chocolate chips, and candy bars broken into different size pieces
* Rice Krispies cereal
* Oreos or other similar cookies, crushed into fine pieces
* spoon
* milk

SEDIMENTARY SUCCESSION TREAT

Sedimentary rocks are sometimes made up of different layers that form in different environments. Over millions of years, the sea level rises and lowers, creating different environments in the same place. Use your imagination and yummy ingredients to make a sedimentary rock you can eat!

Imagine you are standing in a river that flows into the ocean. The river contains pebbles, gravel, sand, and mud that are deposited near where you are standing.

1 In the bottom of the cup, place a layer of large and small pieces of candy bars, chocolate chips, and M&Ms. This represents different-sized sediments from a river.

2 Imagine the sea level rises and now you're standing on a beach. What are you standing on? Put a layer of Rice Krispies into your cup to represent sand.

3 Imagine the sea level rises again. You're still in the same place, but 10 feet underwater! Put a layer of crushed Oreos in the cup. to represent the mud that settles at the bottom of the ocean.

4 Imagine the sea level goes down, then goes down again. Put a layer of Rice Krispies in the cup to represent beach sand, then a layer of large and small pieces of candy, chocolate chips, and M&Ms to represent the river sediments.

5 Press down the layers in your cup to represent the compression from the weight of sediments. Pour milk into the cup to represent water with minerals that cements sediments together into rock.

6 Look at the layers from the side. You should see rocks on the bottom, then sandstone, then mudstone, then sandstone, and rocks on top. Draw and label the layers in your science journal. Now dig in!

YUM!

THINGS TO NOTICE: All of these sediments were deposited in the same place, but in different environments. If the sea level rose again, what layer would be deposited next? If you saw the face of a cliff with layers of sand, then mud, then sand, then mud, what might that tell you about changes in the sea level over time?

THE LAW OF SUPERPOSITION

One of the concepts in geology is the **law of superposition**. This says that sedimentary layers are deposited with the oldest on the bottom and the youngest on top. If you started hiking in the valley and saw the youngest rock, then saw the oldest rock with seashells higher up on the mountain, would this still follow the law of superposition? Are older rocks always lower in elevation than younger rocks?

MAKE YOUR OWN MOUNTAIN

SUPPLIES

* at least 3 colors of play clay
* butter knife
* rolling pin
* small seashells or plastic animals
* small human figure (optional)

Rocks and fossils are deposited in an orderly fashion, with the oldest on the bottom and youngest on top. But forces in the earth sometimes move rocks and their fossils into different positions. Try this activity to see how that happens.

1 Roll out each color of clay to about 6 inches wide and ¼-inch thick. These are your layers of rocks.

2 Push the shells or plastic animals into one of the layers of clay. This layer represents the rock that forms at the bottom of an ocean, and it is the oldest rock. Stack the layers of clay, with the oldest layer of clay on the bottom.

3 With the layers flat on the table, push from both sides. If the clay sticks to the table, lift the middle up into a fold. Your hands are like the pushing forces in the earth that squeeze continents together. The middle is a mountain pushing up from the pressure.

4 Slice off the top at an angle exposing the seashells or animals. This is what happens when rocks are worn away, or eroded, by wind and rain.

THINGS TO NOTICE: If you have a human figure, place it next to the mountain and imagine you're on a hike. If you come upon one of those seashells, what might you think?

CHAPTER 2

CLUES TO THE PAST

Paleontologists use clues from fossils and rocks to find out about ancient life and what happened to it. When they find a fossil, they do a lot of detective work to figure out when the organism lived. Paleontologists want to know what the organism looked like. What did it eat, how did it move, and what environment did it live in? It's a fascinating puzzle!

HOW OLD IS THAT FOSSIL?

First, scientists want to know how old a fossil is. They figure this out by determining the age of the rock that contains the fossil.

?

INVESTIGATE!

Why is it important to study both the fossil and the area around the fossil for clues?

numerical age: the age of a rock or fossil, usually in millions of years.

relative age: the age of a rock or fossil relative to other rocks or fossils.

radiometric dating: a method to determine the numerical age of a rock or fossil. It uses known rates of radioactive decay.

atom: a small particle of matter. Atoms are the extremely tiny building blocks of everything.

radioactive decay: the breakdown of an atom into another kind of atom.

WORDS TO KNOW

Scientists use two different types of ages when looking at rocks with fossils. It can be either the numerical age or the relative age.

One of the best ways to determine the numerical age of a rock is to use radiometric dating. Everything contains atoms. But some materials contain atoms that experience radioactive decay. These radioactive atoms, called parent atoms, lose particles and become a new kind of atom called a daughter atom.

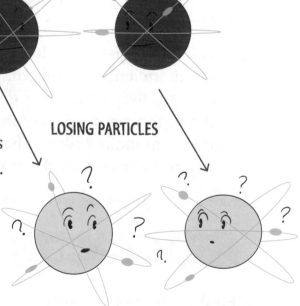

PARENT ATOMS

LOSING PARTICLES

Each kind of parent atom decays at a rate that can be predicted. Scientists can measure how many of the parent atoms are left in the rock compared with the daughter atoms. This helps them to estimate the age of the fossil.

DAUGHTER ATOMS

Scientists can sometimes measure parent and daughter carbon atoms in the remains of plants and animals to tell how long ago the organism died. This is called radiocarbon dating. It only works for materials that are less than about 40,000 years old. That sounds very old. But, as you've learned, it's just a tiny slice in the history of living things.

Most radiometric dating is done on igneous rocks. It gives the age when molten rock cooled to form a solid rock. But because organisms can't live at temperatures high enough to melt rock, fossils aren't found in igneous rocks.

radiocarbon dating: a type of radiometric dating that applies to material that was once living. It can only be used for materials that are about 40,000 years old or younger.

igneous rock: rock that forms from cooling magma. Magma is melted rock below the surface of the earth.

WORDS TO KNOW

Nearly all fossils form in sedimentary rocks, but scientists can't easily date when those rocks formed. Sedimentary rocks are made up of parts of other rocks. So radiometric dating gives the age of the original igneous rock, not the sedimentary rock.

What if scientists find out the age of the igneous rocks above a fossil, which are younger, and below a fossil, which are older? That gives the maximum and minimum age of the fossil.

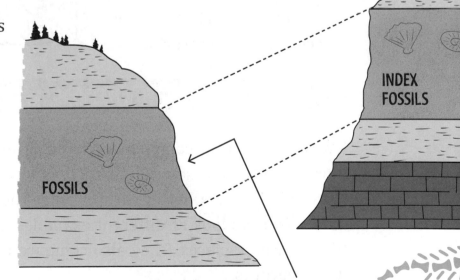

FOSSILS

INDEX FOSSILS

SANDSTONE KNOWN TO BE BETWEEN 300 AND 320 MILLION YEARS OLD

Another method to discover the age of a fossil is to use index fossils. What if we know the age of a type of fossil from one place? Then we can correlate, or match, that fossil with rocks in other places to date the rocks. This type of fossil is called an index fossil.

Index fossils appear for only a short period of time in geological terms. But they are commonly found in many places around the world.

Fossils of sea creatures can be found in the middle of the United States. This shows us that the ocean once covered the interior of North America.

HOW DO WE KNOW WHAT ORGANISMS WERE LIKE?

It's rare to find a complete skeleton of an organism. It's even more rare to find soft tissue such as skin or muscles or plant material. To get a better idea of what these organisms looked like, scientists look at different examples of the same animal to fill in missing pieces. They also compare the animal to present-day creatures.

A skeleton gives the overall size of an animal, but one skeleton by itself can be misleading about a species. What assumptions might we make if we observe the skeleton of a baby animal and think it is an adult? Only by comparing many clues can scientists get a true picture of a species.

There are several ways paleontologists determine what an animal looked like.

* The way bones fit together and the shape of the bones can tell how an animal moved. For example, the shape of the backbone can show whether an animal walked upright or on all fours.

* Bones have scars and ridges that show where the muscles were attached. This can help show the size of the muscles.

* The size and shape of teeth tell us about what the animal ate, and whether it was a predator.

* The size of the skull shows the size of the brain. Large eye holes indicate large eyes, which means the animal had good vision.

WORDS TO KNOW

predator: an animal that hunts other animals for food.

25

herd: a large group of animals.

climate: the average weather patterns in an area over a long period of time.

ecosystem: a community of organisms that interact with each other and their environment.

WORDS TO KNOW

Trace fossils can tell us even more about an animal. For example, tracks can show if an animal traveled in herds or if it fought with other animals.

Footprints can show how heavy the animal was and whether it walked upright or on all fours. The contents of an animal's stomach show what foods it ate. Impressions of skin show if the animal had scales or feathers. Impressions of leaves, bark, and roots show the structure of a plant. Small amounts of chemicals such as copper indicate the color of skin or feathers.

At some points in time, the entire earth has been warm, with no glaciers. At other times, such as now, there have been large areas of permanent ice.

Paleontologists look back to piece together the whole picture: What the land looked like, the climate, and all of the plants and animals and microscopic life that interacted together in an ecosystem. That's a big project and one that will probably never be finished!

INVESTIGATE!

It's time to consider and discuss: Why is it important to study both the fossil and the area around the fossil for clues?

MAKING TRACKS

Animal tracks look different depending on what the animal looked like and what it was doing. Make your own tracks and see how they change with what you do.

1 Pick a time after it rains and walk next to your friend across the sand or mud. Measure the length and depth of each of your footprints. Measure the distance between prints. Record your measurements in your science journal.

2 Smooth out your footprints and run across the surface. Examine the footprints and repeat the measurements.

3 Try other ways of moving, such as hopping, carrying heavy objects, play fighting, and pushing back and forth. Find some dry sand or dirt, and try making tracks there. Each time, examine and measure the tracks and compare how they are different from the set of tracks you made by just walking.

THINGS TO NOTICE: If you saw some of these tracks, what might they tell you about what happened? For example, what was the difference between the tracks where one of you chased the other and the tracks where you were play-fighting?

SUPPLIES

* an area with sand or mud at least 3 feet by 6 feet, such as the beach, a sandbox, or a muddy area
* a friend
* measuring tape or ruler
* heavy objects such as books or large rocks
* science journal and pencil

RADIOACTIVE DATING

Scientists determine the age of rocks and fossils by measuring different kinds of atoms in the rock. Use popcorn to try your own radiometric dating and enjoy a yummy treat!

SUPPLIES

* marker
* 7 or more small bags of unpopped microwave popcorn
* microwave oven
* 5 pieces of paper
* science journal and pencil
* graph paper
* a friend

1 Using the marker, label five of the bags of popcorn with the following: *0 seconds*, *10 seconds*, *20 seconds*, *30 seconds*, and *40 seconds*.

2 Place each bag, one at a time, in the microwave and set the timer for 2 minutes. As soon as the popcorn begins popping, start counting the seconds. After the number of seconds marked on the bag, turn the microwave off and remove the bag. For example, remove the *0 seconds* bag after the first pop.

3 After the bags have cooled down, open each bag and spread the contents on separate pieces of paper. For each bag, count the number of unpopped kernels and popped corn.

4 Record the results in your science journal. Include the bag number, the number of unpopped kernels, and the number of popped corn. You can organize your data in a table like this.

Bag	Unpopped	Popped
0 seconds		
10 seconds		
20 seconds		
30 seconds		
40 seconds		

5 Plot the results on the graph paper. The horizontal axis should be the time, from zero to 50 seconds. The vertical axis should be the percent of kernels that popped, from 0% at the bottom to 100% at the top. To get the percent of kernels that popped for each bag, divide the number of popped corn by the total number of unpopped kernels and popped corn, then multiply by 100.

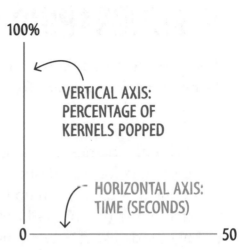

$$\frac{\text{Popped Corn}}{\text{Unpopped Kernels} + \text{Popped Corn}} \times 100 = \text{Percentage of Popped Corn}$$

6 Draw a line through all of the points that you have plotted.

7 Have a friend pop another bag of popcorn for a different time, such as 15 seconds or 25 seconds, without telling you how long. Count the kernels and popped corn, and see if you can guess the amount of time it was popped by using your chart. Now you pop another bag and have your friend guess the time it popped for.

WHAT'S HAPPENING? The unpopped kernels represent the parent atoms in a rock. The popped corn represents the daughter atoms. Just as with your popcorn, the more parent atoms or unpopped kernels there are, the younger the rock.

Do you see a curve to the graph that you made? Radioactivity decreases over time because the fewer parents you have, the slower you lose them. The same is true for the popcorn once it gets going.

STRATIGRAPHIC SEQUENCE

You can see how relative dating works by putting layers of rock into order from oldest to youngest.

SUPPLIES

* a friend
* construction paper of 5 different colors
* two or more plastic containers
* sand and dry soil

1 Write the names of different types of fossils on different colors of construction paper. Make three identical sets. You can go to one of the websites listed at the end of this book to see what the fossils might look like. Draw pictures of the fossils too.

- Red: Trilobites, 504 to 460 million years ago

- Yellow: Brachiopods, 485 to 419 million years ago

- Blue: Graptolites A, 477 million years ago

- Green: Crinoids, 465 to 323 million years ago

- Purple: Corals, 458 to 252 million years ago

- Orange: Graptolites B, 453 million years ago

- Black: Ammonoids, 372 to 359 million years ago

2 You and your friend each fill a plastic container with a layer of sand. Bury three different colors of paper in the sand, representing different fossils. Make sure the time periods for the fossils overlap. Don't show each other which fossils you have chosen.

3 Exchange containers and excavate the fossils. Use logic to figure out the age range of your sand. You can repeat steps 2 and 3 if you like.

4 Together, place a layer of sand in the container and bury one or more fossils in the sand. This will be your oldest layer. Next, place a layer of dry soil and bury more fossils. Alternate sand and soil until you can't use any more combinations of fossils. Make sure the layers go from oldest to youngest.

THINK ABOUT IT: Your papers represent index fossils that can be used to figure out the age of a rock. Which of the fossils would make good index fossils? Which ones wouldn't make good index fossils? Why? What's the greatest number of these fossil species you can have in a layer?

A WHALE OF A FIND!

Sometimes paleontologists are really lucky and find evidence of animals interacting with other animals or their environment. In North Carolina, scientists found a fossil of a whale rib about 3 to 4 million years old. What was really interesting was what scientists could figure out from the rib: The whale had been attacked by a shark and died about two to six weeks after the attack. How could they tell? The rib had three tooth marks about 2.4 inches apart, which must have come from a large shark that lived at that time. Scientists could tell that the whale lived afterward because the bone was covered by a thin layer of bone that forms after an infection. They know this layer of bone doesn't last very long before it is replaced by stronger bone.

You can read an article about the discovery and see pictures of the fossil here. Would you categorize this as a trace fossil or a body fossil?

KEYWORD PROMPTS

whale rib fossil North Carolina

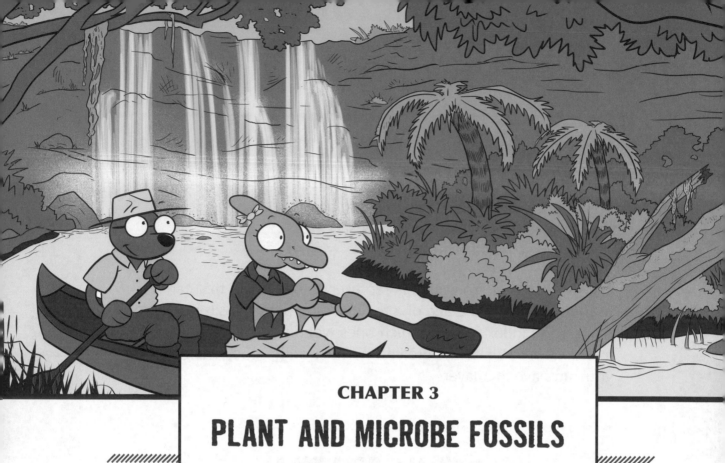

CHAPTER 3

PLANT AND MICROBE FOSSILS

Plants and microbes are the foundation of life on Earth. Without microbes, plants wouldn't exist, and without plants, animals wouldn't exist! Humans are animals too, and we also depend on plants and microbes.

THE FIRST FOSSILS—STINKY MICROBES!

If you could use a time machine to go back to the first billion years of the earth's history, you wouldn't last long. Volcanoes spewed toxic gases. Asteroids and comets smashed into the earth. There was no oxygen.

WORDS TO KNOW

? INVESTIGATE!

What are some of the different ways humans depend on plants?

microbe: another word for microorganism.

toxic: something that is poisonous.

Things got a bit better around 3.5 billion years ago. That's when life first appeared. Microorganisms called cyanobacteria grew. Cyanobacteria aren't like the plants you might grow in your garden or see in the park. But they do use sunlight and carbon dioxide to make energy in a process called photosynthesis. For about 2 billion years, cyanobacteria and other bacteria were the only life on Earth.

Cyanobacteria grow in thin mats. The mats are sticky and trap sediments in layers that look like leaves on a cabbage. Later, when the microbes die, the sediments are cemented together to form a mounded rock called a stromatolite.

cyanobacteria: microbes that are blue-green in color and use photosynthesis.

photosynthesis: the process by which green plants and some microorganisms use sunlight, water, and carbon dioxide to make sugars that they use for food.

stromatolite: a rocky mass made of sediments trapped by mats of bacteria.

WORDS TO KNOW

Although cyanobacteria are still around today, animals eat them before they form stromatolites. But, in far distant times, cyanobacteria grew like crazy in shallow oceans.

You can see pictures of stromatolites here.

KEYWORD PROMPTS

stromatolites photo Indiana 🔍

chloroplasts: tiny structures in the cell of a green plant where photosynthesis takes place.

atmosphere: the blanket of air surrounding the earth.

Why do we care about cyanobacteria that lived so very long ago? Without cyanobacteria, there would be no trees, no insects, no horses, no dinosaurs, and no people. There would be just lots and lots of microbes.

Cyanobacteria were the first organisms to make energy from sunlight. Scientists think that long ago, cyanobacteria began to live inside other cells as chloroplasts. These are the parts of plants that allow them to photosynthesize. Plants wouldn't exist without chloroplasts.

Cyanobacteria were the first organisms to produce oxygen from photosynthesis. Oxygen changed our atmosphere forever. Next time you take a big breath of air, thank cyanobacteria!

Today, cyanobacteria can be a problem when they appear in large amounts in lakes and ponds. They produce a toxin that is harmful to people.

INVASION!

About 450 million years ago, green algae invaded the land. Up until then, except for some microbes, life existed only in the oceans.

Land plants enjoyed more sunlight. But they had to evolve to be strong enough to support themselves. They needed to transport water from roots to leaves without drying out.

The first land plants were ferns, horsetails, and club mosses. Some plants then evolved to use seeds to reproduce. The first seed-bearing plants were conifers, followed by flowering plants. All of these types of plants are still around today. Look out your window. Can you find examples?

Today, club mosses live as tiny plants on forest floors. But millions of years ago, club mosses could grow 90 feet tall in just 10 years. Some ferns were 50 feet tall!

PLANT FOSSILS

How do we know what plants were on the earth long ago? The same way we know about animals—fossils!

Trees can turn into petrified wood. Sometimes, when a tree or other woody plant dies and falls to the ground, it's quickly covered by ash or sediments.

WHY WAS THE TREE SO STIFF?

HA HA HA

Because it was petrified!

groundwater: water contained underground in the tiny spaces in soil and sediment.

organic: something that is or was living, such as animals, wood, grass, and insects.

The oldest evidence of flowers on plants comes from a piece of amber 100 million years old. It has 18 flowers trapped inside, some in the process of making new seeds!

Groundwater containing minerals flows through those sediments. It soaks the wood over a very long period of time. The minerals slowly replace the organic fibers of wood and turn it to stone. Minerals that remain in the stone give the petrified wood amazing colors.

Another type of fossil is amber. This is fossilized tree resin. Amber often contains the remains of animals.

ANCIENT MEAT-EATING PLANT

In 2014 in Russia, a fossil of a **carnivorous** plant was found from about 35 to 47 million years ago! The plant had hairs with a sticky fluid to trap unlucky insects. Scientists had found other parts of carnivorous plants before, but these were the first fossils of the trapping parts of a carnivorous plant to be found.

You can see a picture of the carnivorous plant fossil trapped in amber.

KEYWORD PROMPTS

carnivorous plant amber Russia 🔍

carnivorous: feeding on insects or other animals.

Look in your neighborhood for a pine tree or other conifer. You might see a sticky substance dripping down the tree bark. That's the resin. Insects, spiders, and parts of plants get stuck in it and can't escape. The resin hardens from exposure to light and air and slowly turns to amber, preserving whatever is trapped inside.

WORDS TO KNOW

peat: a brown, soil-like material that contains partially decayed plant matter.

plankton: microscopic organisms drifting in bodies of water.

FOSSIL FUELS, OIL, AND NATURAL GAS

Oil, natural gas, and coal are used to power our cars and heat homes. These fuels come from fossils.

ANCIENT SWAMP

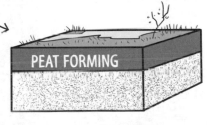

PEAT FORMING

Coal is formed when plant matter falls into swampy water and turns into a slimy brown mush called peat. Over time, mud and sand covers the peat and presses down. The water is squeezed out, and the peat heats up and changes into coal.

SEDIMENTS   PRESSURE

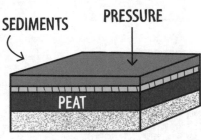

PEAT

Oil and natural gas form when tiny sea creatures called plankton die. They fall to the ocean floor and form a sludge of organic material. Over time, the organic sludge is covered by sediments such as sand and mud. With time, heat and pressure turn the material into oil and natural gas.

INCREASED PRESSURE

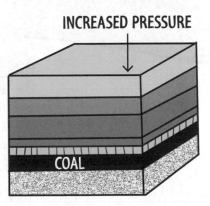

COAL

? INVESTIGATE!

It's time to consider and discuss:
What are some different ways humans depend on plants?

37

EDIBLE AMBER

Animals or plants can become trapped in tree resin, which fossilizes to become amber. Make your own yummy amber!

Caution: An adult needs to help with the boiling water.

SUPPLIES
* bowl
* package of peach or orange Jell-o or gelatin
* 2 cups boiling water
* large spoon
* ice cube tray
* cooking spray
* Swedish Fish or gummy candies in the shape of animals

1 Place the gelatin mix in the bowl. With an adult's help, carefully pour in the boiling water. Stir for 2 minutes until it's completely dissolved.

2 Lightly spray the ice cube tray with cooking spray. Carefully pour the Jell-o mixture into the ice cube tray and place in the refrigerator.

3 When the Jell-o is almost set, push the gummy candies part way into the Jell-o. Put the tray back in the refrigerator for a few hours.

4 When the Jell-o is firm, turn the ice cube tray upside down and release the Jell-o onto a plate.

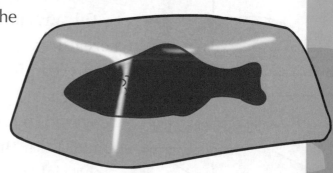

WHAT'S HAPPENING?
Examine your amber fossils. Can you see the gummy candy? The candy is like an animal trapped in amber.

PETRIFIED CELERY

Wood has pores that can carry minerals. The minerals can harden to become petrified wood. Try this activity to see how water flows through pores in plants.

SUPPLIES

* clear drinking glass or jar
* water
* red or blue food coloring
* celery stalks with leaves
* science journal and pencil

1 Fill the jar about a quarter full of water. Place 10 or more drops of food coloring in the water.

2 Cut a stalk of celery without removing the leaves. Look at the cut end. Do you see small holes? These are the pores that carry water in the plant. Place the celery into the jar, cut end down.

3 Let the celery sit for a whole day. Check the celery every few hours and draw what you see happening in your science journal. How long does it take for the food coloring to reach the leaves? Take the celery out and look at the cut end again. What do you see? Draw the image in your science journal.

Petrified tree trunks as long as 190 feet have been found in the Petrified Forest National Park.

WHAT'S HAPPENING? Plants have internal pores that help carry water throughout the plant. These pores are pretty easy to see in celery. The colored water is like groundwater with minerals that fills the pores of buried tree trunks. During petrification, the minerals harden before the trunk has rotted away so the details of the trunk and the pores are preserved.

SUPPLIES

* tree or plant leaves that haven't dried out, in different colors if possible
* hard work surface that won't dent
* newspaper
* white paper
* paper towels
* hammer

PLANT IMPRINT

Sometimes plants become fossilized by leaving behind a thin film of black carbon, called carbonization. Make a beautiful imprint of a leaf using a similar process.

1 Cover your work surface with newspaper and place the paper on top. Arrange the leaves on the paper and cover with two paper towels.

2 Gently hammer everywhere the leaves are. Then hammer a little harder, still being careful to tap everywhere. Hammer again, but this time only tap half of the area. Remove the paper towels and peel away the leaves.

WHAT'S HAPPENING? In nature, plants sometimes are reduced to a fossilized shiny black film on rocks. This is called carbonization. Hammering on the leaves transfers the color of the leaves onto the paper, which is similar to the process of carbonization. Are the colors stronger on the half where you hammered more? Why do you think that happened? When a plant is carbonized, what might cause it to look darker?

carbonization: the conversion of organic matter into a carbon film.

SUPPLIES

* 2-liter bottle
* scissors
* plastic wrap
* water
* sand
* plant leaves
* small sticks
* mud
* pie pan
* newspaper
* table knife
* science journal and pencil

MAKE YOUR OWN PEAT

Peat forms when plants decay in swampy water. Later, the peat is squeezed and heated to form coal. Try making your peat in a similar way!

1 With an adult's help, cut off the top of the soda bottle and remove any labels. Line the inside with plastic wrap. Pour in about 3 inches of water.

2 Add 2 inches of sand and then 2 inches of leaves and sticks. Cover the leaves with water and add 2 inches of mud.

3 Place the bottle on the pie pan and let sit for 2 weeks.

4 Have an adult help you poke 10 holes near the bottom of the bottle. Press down on the top of your layers to drain the water. Place it in a warm area. Press down on the materials each day.

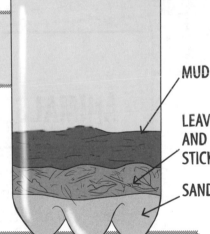

MUD

LEAVES AND STICKS

SAND

5 After several days, when the materials are dry, lift the contents out of the bottle by pulling on the plastic wrap. Set it on newspaper and gently break apart the layers. What does it look like? Record your observations in your science journal.

It takes about a 20-foot layer of plants to become a 10-foot layer of peat, which then becomes a 1-foot layer of coal.

CHAPTER 4

ANIMALS, INCLUDING HUMANS!

All life started in the sea. That's where animals first evolved. The first animals appeared around 600 million years ago and had soft bodies. They were similar to present-day worms, jellyfish, and sponges.

Beginning in the Cambrian period 541 million years ago, the number and types of animals exploded. Worms, creatures with shells, corals, and jointed creatures quickly evolved. Trilobites are some of the early animals from the sea.

? INVESTIGATE!

How has the earth's environment influenced how animals have evolved?

Ammonites were very common and are used as index fossils. These invertebrates had soft bodies. They are related to squid and octopuses, but lived in spiral shells.

Trilobites were animals divided into many segments, like today's arthropods. There were more than 10,000 kinds of trilobites living all over the world. They shed their shells frequently as they grew, which is why we find so many of their fossils!

Fish were the first animals with backbones. These vertebrates began to appear around 530 million years ago. The first fish didn't have jaws and didn't even have fins to help them steer. Fish with jaws and fins evolved later.

TRILOBITE FOSSILS

invertebrate: an animal without a backbone.

arthropod: an invertebrate animal with a skeleton on the outside of its body. It has a segmented body and jointed legs. Insects and spiders are arthropods.

vertebrate: an animal with a backbone.

WORDS TO KNOW

Half of all vertebrate species today are fish!

GIANT DRAGONFLIES

Imagine a dragonfly with a wingspan of more than 2 feet! *Meganeura* lived about 300 million years ago. How did it get so big? Insects can only get to a certain size because of the way oxygen is carried through their bodies. When *Meganeura* flew, the atmosphere contained more oxygen than today, which might have helped it attain its super size.

ONTO THE LAND

The first land animals were millipedes, mites, centipedes, and worms, followed by scorpions and insects. Some of these early creepy-crawlies included a millipede called *Pneumodesmus,* which was the oldest land animal and measured about 1⅜ inches long.

The oldest insect, *Rhyniognatha*, lived more than 400 million years ago and was similar to modern-day flying insects. And, of course, cockroaches have lived on the earth for more than 350 million years!

Once plants and arthropods had expanded onto the land, there were some advantages for other animals to live there, too. There was lots of space, plenty of plants and arthropods to eat, and no predators. Fish that evolved to live on land became the first four-legged creatures, called amphibians. These animals are cold-blooded.

Tiktaalik, nicknamed the "fishapod," was a bridge between fish and amphibians. It had scales and fins like a fish, but also leg-like bones in its fins that allowed it to briefly move on land. It laid its eggs in water.

WORDS TO KNOW

amphibian: a vertebrate animal, such as a frog or salamander, that needs sunlight to keep warm and shade to stay cool. It lays its eggs in water.

cold-blooded: animals such as snakes that have a body temperature that varies with the surrounding temperature.

Some amphibians evolved into reptiles. These animals could venture farther onto the land, where there wasn't as much competition for food. Reptiles have scaly skin to keep them from drying out and they lay an egg with a harder shell that contains liquid. Eventually, a branch of reptiles evolved into mammals.

MAMMALS TAKE OVER

Mammals lived at the same time as dinosaurs, but the mammals then were no bigger than rats! When the dinosaurs became extinct, mammals greatly expanded in number and types of species.

Mammals have hair to insulate their bodies and are warm-blooded. This means they don't depend on the sun for energy. They can live in almost any environment. Mammals spread across the earth, took to the air as bats, and went back to the water as whales and other sea mammals.

The oldest mammal is probably *Adelobasileus* from 225 million years ago. It was the size of a mouse and likely hunted for insects at night in trees.

Mammoths and mastodons are extinct members of the elephant family. Woolly mammoths have been found in Siberia in northern Asia, frozen solid in ice. Some of these mammoths are 40,000 years old! Hair, bones, skin, muscles, and even what they last ate are preserved.

WORDS TO KNOW

warm-blooded: animals such as humans that don't depend on the temperature around them to stay warm.

45

HUMANS

Prehistoric humans weren't the biggest or fastest predators, but they had something special—a powerful brain. About 65 million years ago, early primates appeared.

The earliest human ancestors appeared around 4 million years ago. The most famous fossils of these is "Lucy." This is a partial skeleton of a 3-million-year-old female found in what is present-day Ethiopia. She walked upright, but was only 3 feet 7 inches tall.

"LUCY" IS DISPLAYED IN THE BRITISH MUSEUM

The first humans appeared as early as 2.8 million years ago. What makes us human? We walk upright. We use tools. We use fire, symbols, and language. All human species are part of the genus *Homo*. There have been at least 12 human species, although there's only one human species alive today—*Homo sapiens*. Modern humans arrived on the scene as recently as 195,000 years ago. They lived first in Africa, then spread throughout the world.

Some scientists think that humans evolved because of climate change. As the climate in Africa became drier, the forests disappeared. Our ancestors had to learn to survive in grasslands.

primates: mammals that have large brains, nails on the hands and feet, and a short snout. Apes, monkeys, chimpanzees, and humans are primates.

genus: a group of organisms that consists of one or more species.

climate change: changes to the average weather patterns in an area during a long period of time.

WORDS TO KNOW

? INVESTIGATE!

It's time to consider and discuss: How has the earth's environment influenced how animals have evolved?

DRAGONFLY PIN

Make a colorful dragonfly pin and imagine a giant dragonfly with a wingspan of more than 2 feet!

1 Cut two pieces of plastic in the shape of wings shown below.

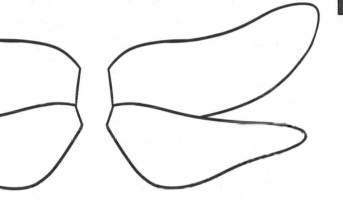

2 Paint the popsicle stick in different colors. Lightly paint the plastic in similar colors.

The biggest land mammal ever was the *Indricotherium*. Now extinct, it was a 25-foot-long rhinoceros weighing 18 tons!

3 Place one plastic wing over the other so they cross in the middle. Glue both pieces to the popsicle stick about a third of the way from one end.

THINGS TO NOTICE: Your dragonfly is a little larger than a modern dragonfly. Imagine a dragonfly from 300 million years ago that has a wingspan of more than 2 feet! Do you think it would fly differently than today's dragonflies? Why?

SUPPLIES

* thin but stiff, clear plastic, similar to cookie packaging
* scissors
* popsicle stick
* tempera paint in two or more colors
* glue

MAKE YOUR OWN FOSSIL

Try this activity to get an idea of how a fossil forms.

Caution: NEVER pour plaster down the sink.

1 Spread out newspaper on a counter or outside. In the plastic cup, add together 2 spoonfuls of plaster of Paris for every 1 spoonful of water. Add enough until the cup is about half full. Stir with the plastic spoon until smooth. Let the plaster set for a minute.

2 Spread a thin coat of petroleum jelly onto the object you are making an imprint of. Press the object face down halfway into the plaster. Leave the edges of the object out of the plaster so you can get it out again. Let it stay there until the plaster is firm.

3 Carefully remove the object. You can cut away the cup if needed. Let the plaster continue to dry for at least 30 minutes, maybe more if the day is humid. You now have a plaster mold.

4 In another cup, mix two parts plaster of Paris and one part water. Add paprika or food coloring if you want.

5 Pour the plaster into your mold. Let it dry thoroughly, about 2 hours or overnight. This is a plaster cast.

SUPPLIES

* newspaper
* large disposable plastic or paper cups
* plaster of Paris, from the hardware or craft store
* water
* plastic spoon
* petroleum jelly
* seashell, plastic egg, leaf, or other distinctive shape
* food coloring or paprika (optional)
* fine sandpaper

6 Carefully remove the cast from the mold. You can make more casts from the same mold if you like. When you're done, you can use fine sandpaper to smooth the surface, and paint your fossil cast.

THINGS TO NOTICE: When you press the object into the wet plaster, it's like the first step in a real fossil being made. Do you think it would take more or less time for a real fossil to form? What other kinds of objects would make good fossils? Why?

HOMO SAPIENS' BEST FRIEND

Modern humans, or *Homo sapiens*, lived in Europe at the same time as another human species, *Homo neanderthalensis*, called Neanderthals. Neanderthals used fire and made tools and were smart like modern humans. But around 42,000 years ago, Neanderthals began to go extinct, while modern humans grew in number. Some scientists think one reason modern humans out-competed Neanderthals was because of dogs. New evidence shows that we tamed wolves to become dogs around that time. The skulls of dogs have only been found in sites of modern humans. Dogs would have helped humans hunt because they run faster, have a better sense of smell, and help defend against enemies.

SUPPLIES

* small paper cups
* apple juice
* small plastic animals

MAKE YOUR OWN ICE FOSSIL

During ice ages, sometimes animals were caught in ice and their entire bodies were preserved as fossils. The oldest ice that has been found on Earth is about 8 million years old.

1 Place a plastic animal in the cup and cover it halfway with apple juice.

2 Place the cup in the freezer. After it freezes, add more apple juice to cover the plastic animal and put it back in the freezer.

3 When it's completely frozen, take out your ice fossil. Break it from the cup by dropping it on the sidewalk or banging lightly with a spoon. If you need to loosen up the ice, run it under warm water first.

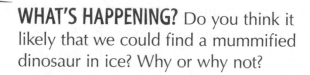

WHAT'S HAPPENING? Do you think it likely that we could find a mummified dinosaur in ice? Why or why not?

In 2013, a team of researchers on a hillside in Ethiopia found what is thought to be the oldest human fossil, 2.8 million years old. An Arizona State University graduate student from Ethiopia named Chalachew Seyoum found a jawbone and five teeth.

 (PS) You can read an article about the discovery and see pictures of the jawbone here.

KEYWORD PROMPTS

oldest human fossil history 🔍

CHAPTER 5

PLANT-EATING DINOSAURS

Dinosaurs were all fierce, huge, and slow-moving, right? Wrong! Dinosaurs came in all shapes and sizes. Some were large and menacing, others were tiny and fearful, and most were quick. Some even had feathers!

THE AGE OF DINOSAURS

Dinosaurs came on the scene during the Mesozoic Era, after the largest extinction on the planet. They roamed the earth for about 160 million years. That's only about 4 percent of the history of life on the earth, but it's 57 times longer than humans have been around.

INVESTIGATE!

How did the bodies of plant-eating dinosaurs help them survive?

carnivore: an animal that eats meat.

herbivore: an animal that eats plants.

The Mesozoic Era is divided into the Triassic, Jurassic, and Cretaceous Periods. During the Triassic Period, there was one huge, C-shaped super continent, with scorching deserts in the middle. Extinction had wiped out many species, so there was room for dinosaurs to evolve. The first dinosaurs were small carnivores that walked on two legs. These were followed by herbivores.

During the Jurassic Period, the super-continent started breaking up and the climate became wetter. Large trees and plants grew and the plant-eating giant dinosaurs evolved. Other reptiles ruled the sea and air.

There were more kinds of dinosaurs than ever during the Cretaceous Period, including *Tyrannosaurus rex*. The continents continued to split up into many different ecosystems, just as we have today.

Dinosaur fossils have been found mainly in the western United States, Argentina, Mongolia, and China, but dinosaurs lived on every continent. They dominated the planet until they all became extinct at the end of the Mesozoic Era.

Fossils of more than 1,000 species of dinosaurs have been discovered all over the world. Many more species will probably be found.

TRIASSIC

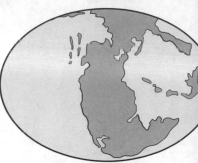

JURASSIC

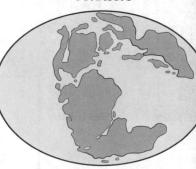

CRETACEOUS

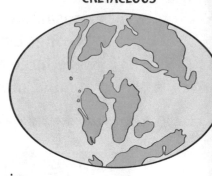

DINOSAUR TYPES

Dinosaurs can be divided into two groups based on the type of hip bones they had. The saurischians are called lizard-hipped dinosaurs. They include all carnivores, called theropods, and all of the huge, long-necked herbivores called sauropods.

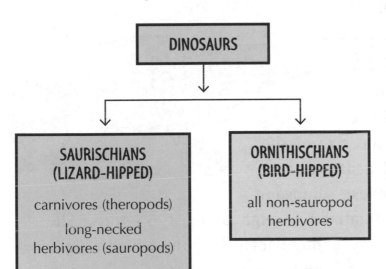

```
            DINOSAURS


SAURISCHIANS              ORNITHISCHIANS
(LIZARD-HIPPED)           (BIRD-HIPPED)

carnivores (theropods)    all non-sauropod
                          herbivores
long-necked
herbivores (sauropods)
```

saurischians: dinosaurs that had a hip structure like lizards, where the pubic bone points forward. All theropods and sauropods are saurischians.

theropods: a group of dinosaurs that walked on two hind legs and included all meat-eaters.

sauropods: a group of plant-eating dinosaurs that walked on four legs and had a long neck and tail.

ornithischians: dinosaurs that had a hip structure like birds, where the pubic bone points down and backward. All plant-eaters that are not sauropods are ornithischians.

WORDS TO KNOW

The second group is the ornithischians, also called bird-hipped dinosaurs. These included nearly all of the plant-eaters that weren't sauropods.

Sauropods were the longest, heaviest, and tallest creatures ever to walk the earth. They had huge, thick legs like tree trunks and long tails that balanced their long necks.

Duck-billed dinosaurs called hadrosaurs chewed food in three directions—back and forth, up and down, and out to the sides.

53

WHY DID THE DINOSAUR CROSS THE ROAD?

HA   HA

HA

Because the chicken hadn't evolved yet!

Sauropods adapted to eating different plants at different heights. It depended on the length and structure of their necks and teeth. Some long-necks couldn't hold their heads up above about 12 feet. These dinosaurs held their necks parallel with the ground and swung them back and forth to graze. Other dinosaurs with very long necks reached up to graze the treetops.

ARGENTINOSAURUS

In the Jurassic Period, sauropods became huge. Some were 10 times the size of the biggest meat-eaters. *Argentinosaurus* is perhaps the heaviest dinosaur discovered so far, estimated to weigh at least 55 tons. The heaviest land animal today is the African elephant, which weighs only 7 tons.

DIPLODOCUS

Diplodocus is the longest dinosaur. We know this from a nearly complete skeleton. It was 108 feet long, with an incredibly long tail made of 80 vertebrae. Scientists think that *Diplodocus* may have snapped its tail like a whip, making a loud booming sound to scare off predators.

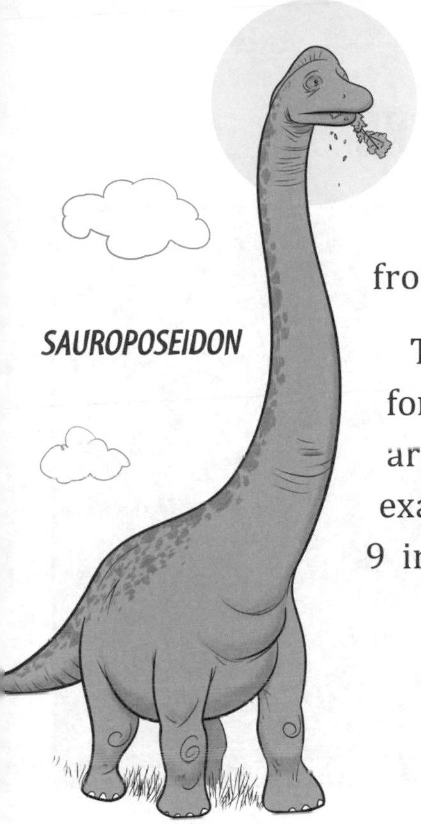

Sauroposeidon is the tallest dinosaur yet discovered. Scientists estimate it could reach 60 feet high, as tall as a six-story building. It had the longest neck of any animal ever—40 feet from head to shoulders.

SAUROPOSEIDON

The ornithischians came in all sorts of shapes and forms. They had a variety of features, including armor, spikes, horns, bony heads, and duckbills. For example, *Pachycephalosaurus* had super-thick skulls 9 inches thick. These skulls might have been used for head-butting or display.

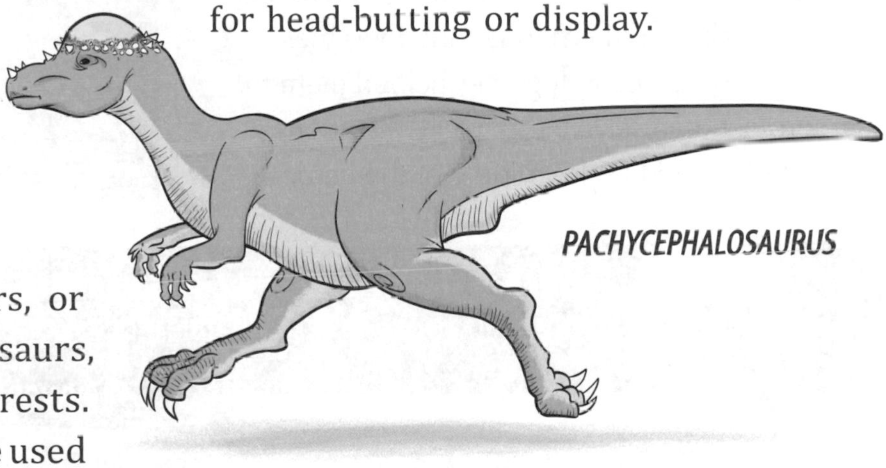

PACHYCEPHALOSAURUS

The hadrosaurs, or duck-billed dinosaurs, had bony head crests. They might have used these to blow air through and make loud sounds like trumpets. This would scare predators or attract a mate.

TRICERATOPS

Triceratops had three large horns on a huge skull up to 8½ feet long. It might have used its powerful head for fighting.

trackway: a pathway of continuous dinosaur footprints.

WORDS TO KNOW

JOIN THE HERD

Trackways, or pathways of continuous dinosaur footprints, show that dinosaurs traveled in herds, often across long distances. The Dinosaur Freeway is a thin layer of rocks that stretches from Colorado into New Mexico. It contains thousands of individual footprints. Plant-eaters needed to eat a lot of food, and moving to different areas allowed them to get the food they needed. Traveling together helped them to protect themselves, especially the young, who traveled in the middle of the herd.

(PS) **You can see pictures of the Dinosaur Freeway here.** What do you notice about the prints?

KEYWORD PROMPTS

Dinosaur Freeway wonders 🔍

DINNERTIME FOR PLANT-EATERS

It's harder to digest plants than meat. Plant-eating dinosaurs had large stomachs and long intestines to help with digestion. This made their bellies quite large. Many plant-eaters walked on four legs to support their big bellies.

Herbivores also had different kinds of teeth. Some were shaped like pencils or spoons to help them eat tough plant leaves. Some plant-eaters had beaks to slice fruits and nuts.

The herbivores didn't have to spend time hunting, but they did have to eat a lot to get all the nutrients they needed. They spent their days eating, and eating, and . . . eating. The largest plant-eaters had to eat a ton of food every day!

ARMORED UP!

The teeth of plant-eaters were good at chewing and grinding plants, but weren't sharp and powerful. They needed other ways of defending themselves. One thing they used was size. Imagine being stepped on by a 50-ton dinosaur!

Smaller dinosaurs ran and hid in burrows or underbrush. Or they used camouflage to make themselves less visible. Some were very fast and could change direction quickly to escape. They traveled in herds, hiding their young in the middle.

Some herbivores had heavy plates and scales like armor that were hard to bite through. Many dinosaurs had long, strong tails they could use to swipe an attacker.

nutrients: substances in food and soil that living things need to live and grow.

camouflage: the colors or patterns that allow a plant or animal to blend in with its environment.

WORDS TO KNOW

Nigersaurus **had about 500 pencil-shaped teeth. They were arranged in rows in the front of its jaw and allowed it to mow down low-growing plants. The jaw was wider than its head and its teeth were replaced every two weeks!**

? INVESTIGATE!

It's time to consider and discuss: How did the bodies of plant-eating dinosaurs help them survive?

57

SUPPLIES

* sturdy bag with handles
* several rocks
* broom or long stick
* science journal and pencil

REALLY LONG NECK

Sauropods had very long necks. How do you think this affected the way they moved? What would it be like to try to walk with a very long neck? Try this to see how it might feel to be a sauropod.

1 Place the rocks into the bag and hold it close to your chest. Then try holding the bag at arm's length.

2 Hang the bag by its handles on the end of the broom. Hold it out in front of you. Which way was easiest to hold the rocks? Which way was hardest? Record your observations in your science journal.

Albertonectes, an ocean-dwelling plesiosaur, had a REALLY long neck, with 76 neck vertebrae! Compare that with nearly all mammals, including humans and giraffes, that have only seven neck vertebrae.

THINGS TO NOTICE: Sauropods had very long necks, but small heads. Why do you think their heads were so small? Could they have easily lifted their head if it were large? Why do you think human necks are short?

DINOSAUR FIGURES

Dinosaurs had different shapes, depending on how they needed to move and what they ate. Try making models of a plant-eater and a meat-eater.

1 For the sauropod, mold the clay into a small mango shape.

2 Break two pencils in half. Insert the pieces as legs into the clay, with the broken end in the clay. Attach a grape-sized piece of clay onto the end of a pencil. Insert the pencil into the clay as the neck, with the grape-sized clay as the head. On the other end, insert a pencil as a tail for balance, pointing straight back. Adjust the length of the tail and neck as needed so the dinosaur balances.

3 For the meat-eater such as *Tyrannosaurus rex*, mold the clay into a shape about the size of a pear with a golf ball attached.

4 Break a pencil in half and insert the two pieces through the head for the heavy jaw. Insert two toothpicks as arms and two pencils as legs. To the bottom of each leg, attach a flattened, grape-sized piece of clay for feet. Insert a pencil as a tail for balance, but position it straight back so it doesn't touch the table. You might have to adjust the position of the legs to get it to balance.

THINGS TO NOTICE: Why do you think dinosaurs had tails? Which animal do you think could move faster, a four-legged sauropod with a long neck or a two-legged *T. rex*?

SUPPLIES

* 2 or more rolls of string
* measuring tape
* scissors
* Post-it notes
* pencil

HOW BIG WERE DINOSAURS?

Dinosaurs came in all sizes. Try this activity to see just how large and small they could be.

1 Find a large area where you can roll out the string, such as a long hallway, sidewalk, or park. Choose a dinosaur from the list below and roll out the string. Measure the length with the measuring tape, then cut the string at the proper length. On the Post-it note, write the name of the dinosaur, length, and whether it's the dino's length or height. Attach it to the base of the string.

2 Continue rolling out lengths for more dinosaurs. Start each one at the same baseline so you can compare lengths. Finish with one for your own height.

Diplodocus (sauropod)	108 feet in length
Sauroposeidon (sauropod)	60 feet in height
one neck bone of *Sauroposeidon*	4 feet 7 inches in length
Micropachycephalosaurus (ornithischian)	1 foot 7 inches in length
skull of *Triceratops* (horned plant-eater)	8 feet 6 inches in length
Tyrannosaurus rex (carnivore)	40 feet in length
Quetzalcoatlus (pterosaur)	36 feet in wingspan
Spinosaurus (carnivore)	50 feet in length
spines of the *Spinosaurus*	7 feet in length
Elasmosaurus (sea monster with long neck)	46 feet in length
claws of *Therizinosaurus* (plant-eater)	3 feet in length

CHAPTER 6
MEAT-EATING DINOSAURS

Dinosaurs and their relatives were some of the largest and most ferocious predators ever to live on the earth. Carnivorous dinosaurs often hunted live prey. They needed weapons to be successful and stay alive. What were some of these weapons?

WEAPONS

The meat-eating dinosaurs had some impressive physical features to help them survive. Claws and teeth were both very important. Claws were sharp and could be up to a foot long. Some dinosaurs called dromaeosaurs had a huge claw on each foot that could slash prey.

WORDS TO KNOW

prey: an animal hunted by a predator for food.

dromaeosaur: the name for dinosaur raptors. Raptors were small- to medium-sized meat-eaters that walked on two legs with long, grasping fingers and a huge claw on each foot.

? INVESTIGATE!

Why did meat-eating dinosaurs come in such a variety of sizes and abilities?

61

Most carnivores had sharp teeth to help them attack and puncture the flesh of prey. They didn't need teeth that could chew because meat is easy to digest. They just tore the flesh from prey and gulped it down!

Their teeth could be as large as bananas and were specialized in size and shape for the type of prey.

Five-year-old Daisy Morris found a fossil of a new species of pterosaur in 2008 on the Isle of Wight, England. The new species was named after her: *Vectidraco daisymorrisae*.

Predators had larger brains than plant-eaters. They needed bigger brains to hunt, to help them understand smells, sights, and sounds. Plant-eaters only had to have enough smarts to catch plants and watch out for predators!

Predators also needed speed to catch their food. All meat-eaters walked on two legs. They were more lightly built than many plant-eaters so they could run faster.

THE GREAT PREDATORS

TROODON

Meat-eating dinosaurs could be as small as a chicken or as large as 50 feet long. Just like predators today, meat-eaters were all a little different.

The *Troodon* had the most smarts of any dinosaur, based on the size of its brain compared to its body. It was as big as a man and had excellent hearing and eyesight.

The *Giganotosaurus* was the largest predator, about 5 feet longer and 3 tons heavier than *T. rex.* It lived in the late Cretaceous Period in Argentina.

GIGANOTOSAURUS

DEINONYCHUS

Deinonychus was a human-sized raptor with short, thick legs and powerful slicing claws. It had a 5-inch sickle-shaped claw on its second toe that it snapped out like a switchblade to slice its prey. It was able to kill prey twice its size and probably hunted in packs. The *Velociraptors* in *Jurassic Park* were based on *Deinonychus*.

Microraptor had two wings on both its arms and legs! It might seem as though having four wings could help you fly better, but *Microraptor* probably just glided between trees.

MICRORAPTOR

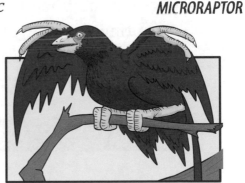

THE KING!

Tyrannosaurus rex is Latin for "tyrant lizard king." It was 40 feet long from snout to tail and probably the most ferocious creature of all time. *T. rex* had eyes the size of oranges, long, curved claws, and about 60 serrated, 12-inch-long pointed teeth. Its bite could rip away 500 pounds of meat in one chomp!

T. REX

T. rex appeared around 68 million years ago, during the Cretaceous Period. So far, we have only found its fossils in the American West. About 3 million years after it appeared, all dinosaurs were wiped out.

A *T. rex* egg was about the size of a basketball and weighed a few pounds. The mother kept her nest covered with plant material to keep the eggs warm. When the babies hatched, they were tiny, probably with downy feathers. A fully grown adult weighed more than 12,000 pounds and had feet more than 2 feet long.

WHAT DO YOU GET WHEN TWO T. REX CRASH THEIR CARS?

HA HA HA

Tyrannosaurus wrecks!

OTHER PREDATORS

Huge reptiles dominated the seas during the Mesozoic Era. Although they lived in the sea, they breathed air, so they had to come to the surface often. They had paddle-like limbs that they used to swim and steer. These sea monsters are classified into three different groups.

Only two fossils of poop, called coprolite, from a tyrannosaurid have been found. The biggest, found in Alberta, Canada, was from an early relative of *T. rex*. It was 2 feet long and 6.5 inches wide!

Plesiosaurs came in two variations. Those with short necks and long heads are called pliosaurs. Those with incredibly long necks and short heads are called elasmosaurs.

Mosasaurs were related to land-dwelling monitor lizards. They could be up to 43 feet long, and had powerful tails.

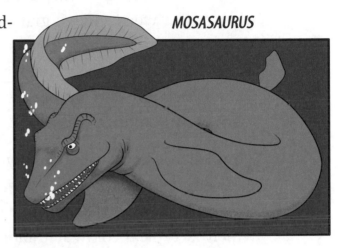

MOSASAURUS

Ichthyosaurs had a shape similar to present-day dolphins. They had long snouts, lots of short, sharp teeth, flippers, and powerful tails. Like dolphins, they could probably swim very fast. Ichthyosaurs gave birth to live young underwater. Several fossils of mothers about to give birth have been found.

FLYING REPTILES

Pterosaurs were the first vertebrate creatures to fly. They could be as small as sparrows or as large as planes. They had hollow bones to reduce weight, large brains, and could see far, just like modern-day birds. But these were reptiles! Pterosaurs had leathery skin and perhaps fur. They probably didn't have feathers. They also could walk on all fours, which helped them launch into the air. Their wings were like four-fingered hands, where the fourth finger was very long and had webbing to form the wing. Most pterosaur fossils have been found in rocks from shallow seas. They glided along the coastline, scooping up fish to eat.

HOW WE WERE WRONG

Scientists used to think that dinosaurs were like giant, sluggish, cold-blooded lizards. In 1975, paleontologist Robert Bakker argued that dinosaurs were warm-blooded and active.

Quetzalcoatlus and its close relative, *Hatzegopteryx*, had wingspans of as much as 36 feet! That's almost the length of a school bus and is the longest wingspan of any creature ever.

Evidence shows that many of them, especially meat-eaters and smaller dinosaurs, were warm-blooded. Some dinosaur fossils have lots of blood vessels, which is typical for warm-blooded animals. We've even found dinosaur fossils in polar regions, where cold-blooded animals can't live.

CHATTER CHATTER

More recent discoveries have changed how we look at dinosaurs. Scientists have taken a fresh look at older discoveries using microscopes and computer modeling.

Scientists know that dinosaurs' legs were positioned underneath them, not out to the side like lizards. They didn't drag their tails, but held them out straight behind them. Tails were used to balance heads and necks.

Feathers have been found on many different kinds of dinosaurs in China and elsewhere. We think they used feathers to keep warm and to identify each other.

An *Anchiornis* fossil contains remains of feathers. Some scientists think it had black and white wings and a red head!

Like all reptiles, dinosaurs laid eggs. But unlike most other reptiles, many dinosaurs built nests and stayed with the eggs until they hatched. There's also evidence that many fed their young until they were big enough to catch their own prey.

? INVESTIGATE!

It's time to consider and discuss:
Why did meat-eating dinosaurs come in such a variety of sizes and abilities?

EARLIEST FLYING DINOSAUR

Archaeopteryx, whose fossils were first discovered in 1863, was the earliest known flying dinosaur. *Archaeopteryx* was covered in feathers like a bird, but it also had a skeleton like a dinosaur, including a long bony tail, a narrow jaw with teeth, and clawed wings. Paleontologists thought they'd discovered a true link between dinosaurs and birds. Even Charles Darwin expressed excitement!

(PS) **You can read a letter Darwin wrote about the discovery.** Does the language sound strange? How is it different from language we use today?

KEYWORD PROMPTS

Darwin correspondence 3905 🔍

BALANCE

Meat-eaters had to catch their prey, but finding the right balance to move fast enough wasn't always easy. Try this activity to see how a meat-eater might have different balance than a sauropod.

1 Tie the paper clip to the string and tape the other end to your shirt just above your belly button. Lean forward with feet apart. The clip should dangle between your feet.

2 Lift one foot but also lean so that the clip dangles over one foot. Put your foot back down. Now lift one foot but don't let the paper clip move. Did you fall down?

3 Lift one leg behind you and lean forward. Now bring your leg down. What happens to the paper clip? Write down your observations in your science journal.

WHAT'S HAPPENING?

The paper clip moves depending on where your center of gravity is. Meat-eaters had to move fast to catch prey, and their bodies had to be in the right position to do that— leaning forward on two legs and balancing with their tails.

MAKE A *T. REX* TOOTH

What did a *T. Rex* tooth look like? Make one and find out!

1 Cover a table with newspaper. Lightly crumple aluminum foil into the shape of a large banana.

2 In the bowl, mix about 1 cup of water to ½ cup flour and stir until there are no lumps. Tear newspaper into strips. Dip a strip in the paste until it's covered. Squeeze off extra paste. Wrap the coated strip around the aluminum foil. Continue wrapping strips until you have two layers of strips on the entire piece. Let dry for a day or two.

3 When it is completely dry, paint if you like.

SUPPLIES

* newspaper
* aluminum foil
* bowl
* flour
* water
* tempera paint (optional)

PREDATOR X VS. GREAT WHITE SHARK

If we could bring fossils to life, who would win in a fight between the great white shark and Predator X, the nickname for *Pliosaurus funkei*?

The Great White Shark	Predator X
nearly 20 feet long	43 feet long
bite that exerted a force of 4,000 pounds	bite that exerted a force of 33,000 pounds
teeth 3 inches long	teeth up to 1 foot long

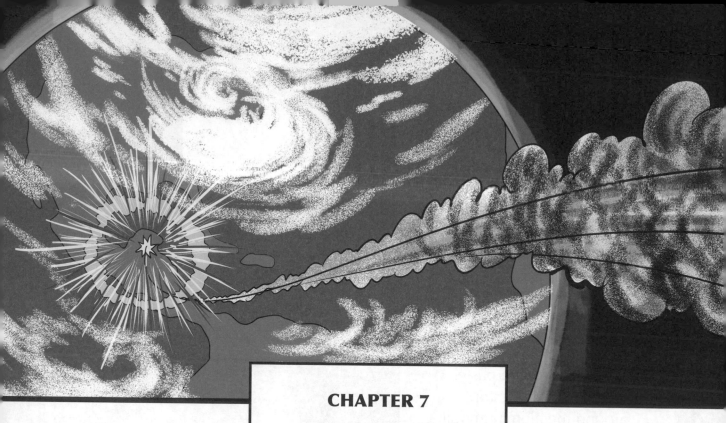

CHAPTER 7

BOOM AND BUST

Scientists used to think that organisms always evolved and became extinct gradually, during long periods of time. Evolution and extinction do happen gradually, but they can also happen very quickly.

EXPLOSION OF LIFE

About 542 million years ago, at the beginning of the Cambrian Period, life changed. Animals went from having simple forms, such as sponges, to representing all of the different animal groups. It happened in about 20 million years. This might sound like a long time, but it's the blink of an eye in the geologic timescale.

? INVESTIGATE!

When one species evolves or becomes extinct, how does that affect other species?

70

This burst of evolution is called the Cambrian explosion. Some of the creatures that evolved in this explosion include creatures with shells. These are molluscs and arthropods such as trilobites. *Opabinia* appeared. This arthropod had five eyes and used a flexible, clawed arm attached to its head to grab prey.

Pikaia gracilens was a creature that looked like a worm but had the beginnings of a backbone. This makes it an ancestor of vertebrates such as us.

The reasons for the Cambrian explosion are complex, but probably include changes in the environment. These include increases in oxygen in the atmosphere. There would have been increased interaction and competition between organisms.

THE BURGESS SHALE

In 1909, a paleontologist named Charles Walcott from the Smithsonian Institution was in British Columbia, Canada, looking for fossils. He found a huge number from the Cambrian Period in one area, called the Burgess Shale. The fossils had the soft parts of the animals as well, which usually decay before they fossilize. Since then, other places with soft-bodied fossils have been found in China and Utah. Long ago, the Burgess Shale was in the deep ocean, where lots of sediment was deposited, so creatures were covered quickly when they died. About 225,000 fossils have been found in the Burgess Shale!

WORDS TO KNOW

background extinction: the constant low-level rate of extinction.

EXTINCTION!

Extinction happens when the last individual of a species dies. Background extinction has gone on throughout history. This is when species become extinct because of many reasons. These can be changes in the environment. Maybe new predators or competitors move in. Or it can happen because of disease, lack of food or nesting sites, or a combination of things. Sometimes a species appears to have become extinct because it has evolved into a new species.

The word *dinosaur* comes from the ancient Greek words *deinos* for "fearfully great" and *sauros* for "lizard."

At other times, large numbers of species go extinct very quickly. When many species become extinct in a short period of time, scientists call it a mass extinction.

Mass extinctions are caused by different things. Large volcanic eruptions can cause massive amounts of hot lava to flow for long periods of time. Volcanoes also spew out lots of ash, poisonous gases, and other gases that can heat up or cool down the earth.

Mass extinction can also happen if a very large meteorite slams into the surface of the earth. It can cause wildfires, earthquakes, and tsunamis. Huge amounts of dust spray into the atmosphere. This blocks much of the sunlight from reaching the planet's surface. Meteorites such as these are very, very rare!

meteorite: a meteor that is not burned up by the earth's atmosphere and hits the earth's surface.

tsunami: a long, high sea wave caused by an earthquake or other disturbance.

WORDS TO KNOW

Climate change can also cause mass extinction. Over geologic time, the earth's climate has changed from ice ages to searing heat and deserts. This affects sea levels and ocean currents. When organisms don't have time to adapt to the changes, a mass extinction can occur.

WHAT COMES AFTER EXTINCTION? Y-tinction!

HA HA HA

WHAT COMES AFTER Y-TINCTION? Z-end!

There have been five major mass extinctions. About 252 million years ago, the Permian Period ended with what's called the Great Dying. Volcanic eruptions in Siberia in northern Russia poured out huge amounts of lava that covered a land area twice the size of Alaska. Poisonous gases and carbon dioxide heated up the planet. About 90 percent of marine life and 70 percent of land species became extinct.

The dinosaurs, pterosaurs, marine reptiles, and many other species were wiped out by another mass extinction about 65 million years ago, at the end of the Cretaceous Period. This extinction probably had multiple causes. These include massive outpourings of lava in what is now India and a large meteorite slamming into the earth.

IS THERE A SIXTH MASS EXTINCTION?

Normally, a few species become extinct every year as background extinction. But right now, there's a much higher rate of extinction going on. Many scientists even think we're entering a sixth mass extinction. They believe that human behavior is a big reason for it. Hunting, clearing large areas of land, overfishing, and climate change are all things that can cause animals to become extinct.

Humans have also worked to bring plants and animals back from near-extinction. Some include black-footed ferrets, condors, and salamanders. What can you do to help the world and the species that live here from going extinct?

  (PS) You can find some tips here.

KEYWORD PROMPTS

save endangered species coalition 🔍

In 1980, a geologist named Walter Alvarez and his physicist father, Luis, found a thin layer of clay with something special in it. The clay had a large amount of an element found in meteorites. This layer was also found in other places around the world.

What was really interesting, is that the clay matched the time when dinosaurs disappeared from the fossil record. Scientists developed the theory that a meteorite had been part of this mass extinction. Some years later, a crater 110 miles in diameter was identified on Mexico's Yucatán Peninsula from the same time.

The amount of energy released when the meteorite hit was about 10,000 times stronger than the energy released by a hurricane in one day. Combined with all of the other stresses from volcanic eruptions, it was too much for many species, including the dinosaurs, to survive.

living fossils: a living species that has changed little from long ago and doesn't have close relatives still alive.

WORDS TO KNOW

LIVING FOSSILS

Living fossils are plants and animals that haven't changed since early geological time. For example, we thought the coelacanth had become extinct shortly before the dinosaurs.

More than 99 percent of all species that have lived on the earth have become extinct.

Then, in December 1938, a fisherman caught one off the coast of South Africa! It looks much like it did more than 400 million years ago, with a hinged joint in its skull that can open wide for large prey.

Sponges appeared about 600 million years ago, and still live today in the oceans. They have very simple bodies full of pores and channels. This allows water to flow through them.

Horseshoe crabs are another example of living fossils. These creatures haven't changed much in the last 445 million years. They're actually closely related to spiders and scorpions.

INVESTIGATE!

It's time to consider and discuss: When one species evolves or becomes extinct, how does that affect other species?

PROJECT TIME!

SUPPLIES

* rock about the size of your palm
* outside area with loose, bare dirt or sand
* science journal and pencil

SMALL ROCK, BIG IMPACT

Scientists think a meteor hitting the earth contributed to the extinction of the dinosaurs. Try this activity to see how scientists might have used clues to figure out the size and direction of the meteor.

1 Stand outside and drop the rock into the dirt from a few inches above the ground. Then stand a few feet away from the dirt and throw the same rock onto the dirt as hard as you can.

2 Compare the mark made from the gentle drop and a hard throw. Which is deeper? What does the ground around it look like?

THINGS TO NOTICE: Scientists can calculate the speed and size of the meteorite that impacted off the coast of Mexico when dinosaurs became extinct. They can also calculate the angle and direction that it came from. This is based on the direction and distance that rocks were sprayed. If you saw just the spray of dirt from your own rock, could you tell which direction the rock had come from?

COLORFUL METEORITE IMPACT

Meteorites create a shock wave when they hit the earth. Try this activity to see what it might have looked like.

SUPPLIES

* newspaper
* large shallow pan or cookie sheet
* whole milk
* food coloring in several colors
* dish soap
* fork or thin stirring stick
* science journal and pencil

1 Spread out newspaper and place the pan on top. Pour a thin layer of milk into the pan to cover the entire bottom of the pan.

2 Add a few drops of food coloring into the center of the pan. Add a few drops of a second color next to the first color.

3 Add a couple drops of dish soap between the colors. What happens?

4 Very gently and slowly swoop the stick or fork through the colors. See if you can get thin tendrils of color swirling around. Look closely at the drop of soap. What do you see?

5 Dump the milk and food color mixture into the sink. Try it again with different colors. What happens if you try it with water or cream instead of milk? Record and draw your observations in your science journal.

WHAT'S HAPPENING? The food coloring zooms to the outside because of the way the soap interacts with the water. When a meteorite hits the earth, a shockwave would radiate outward from the impact, just as the food coloring did.

SUPPLIES

* clear pie pan
* cornstarch
* warm tap water
* spoon
* bright light (100W bulb or brighter)
* science journal and pencil

LAVA COLUMNS

Scientists think huge volcanic eruptions may have contributed to the extinction of dinosaurs. Use cornstarch to see how lava cools to form the rock called basalt.

1 Mix equal parts of cornstarch and water in the pie pan until the pan is about half full. Stir well.

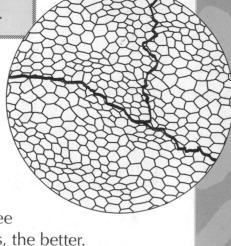

2 Set the pie pan several inches under a bright light or in a sunny window for about a week, or until it is completely dry. Start a scientific method worksheet. What is your hypothesis? What do you think will happen to the cornstarch mixture? You'll first see cracks that break the cornstarch into disconnected shapes. Keep the cornstarch under the light until you see much finer cracks at the top. The longer it dries, the better.

3 Hold the pie plate up and look at the bottom. Do you see shapes? Carefully pry up a few pieces of cornstarch to see if it formed columns. If you don't see columns, let the cornstarch dry longer and try again. Carefully remove from the pan. Look at the bottom of the cornstarch. Do you see any shapes?

WHAT'S HAPPENING? As lava cools, it shrinks and forms cracks. The cracks start out in a random pattern. As they continue to form, the crack pattern becomes hexagonal because hexagons are more stable. A hexagon is a six-sided shape. Scientists use cornstarch and water to study how basalt rock cools and forms columns.

CHAPTER 8
HOW PALEONTOLOGISTS WORK

Paleontologists want to understand the history of life on Earth. They ask big questions about how life evolves and how the planet changes. The core of what a paleontologist does is field work—finding, collecting, and studying fossils.

FROM BURIED IN ROCKS TO MUSEUM EXHIBITS

How does a fossil go from being encased in rocks to watching over the halls of a museum?

Sometimes a fossil is discovered by chance. Most of the time, though, scientists are looking in rock layers where they expect to find fossils.

? INVESTIGATE!

What questions about fossils do you find most interesting?

Paleontologists carefully dig around the fossil using rock picks, chisels, and paintbrushes. They take photographs and make maps of the area.

The fossil and any surrounding rock are wrapped in protective plaster and burlap. Then the fossil and rock are taken to a museum or university laboratory by backpack, truck, or even helicopter!

FOSSIL HUNTING

Finding a fossil of a creature that lived millions of years ago is an amazing experience. Keep your eyes open for fossils in the ground or in riverbeds. Sometimes, stones in buildings or walls can have fossils in them! For an organized fossil hunt, you'll need some supplies.

* goggles

* safety helmet

* protective gloves

* sturdy shoes

* rock hammer

* small chisels

* magnifying glass

* cloth bags, small containers, or Ziploc bags for storing fossils

* labels and pen for labeling containers

* science journal

* fossil field guide and identification book

Remember to always ask the landowner for permission to hunt fossils! Look in places where rocks are exposed, such as around loose boulders or short cliffs. Always wear a safety helmet around cliffs, and be especially careful around taller cliffs that could have dangerous rockfalls.

Look in sedimentary rocks, such as sandstone, shale, or limestone. Sedimentary rocks are often crumbly. Sometimes they have visible grains or layers, like bands of color.

When you find something that you think is a fossil, carefully collect it along with its surrounding rock. Don't forget that you need permission from the landowner. Chisel away the rock around the fossil. Always wear safety goggles to protect your eyes. Label the container with the location and the date. Make more notes about the rocks, conditions, and exact location in your fossil journal.

Back at home, clean the fossil carefully with a soft brush and water. Try to identify the fossil by comparing it with pictures in a field guide or other books.

WHAT DO DINOSAURS HAVE THAT OTHER ANIMALS DON'T? HA HA HA —Baby Dinosaurs.

FINDING THE OLDEST MAMMAL: LUCK AND PERSISTENCE

On a warm day in 1990 in west Texas, Dr. Spencer Lucas and two graduate students, Adrian Hunt and Ken Kietzke, were fossil hunting in a dried-up lake bed of Late Triassic age. They hoped to collect fossils of ostracods, which are animals related to shrimp about the size of the head of a pin. They found an area with lots of tiny bones and shoveled sediment into bags to take back to their lab to sift for fossils.

About a month later, Kietzke walked into Dr. Lucas's office, excited. His sifting had turned up a small skull attached to coprolite, or fossilized poop. The skull was only about as big as the nail on your pinky finger.

At the laboratory, scientists use dental tools and brushes to scrape all of the rock from the fossil.

The three of them studied the skull to determine what kind of animal it was. In vertebrates, the skull attaches to the backbone by knobs at the base of the skull. Mammal skulls have two knobs, but dinosaurs and other reptiles and birds have only one knob.

The skull had two knobs, so it was a mammal! And even more exciting, the fossil had been found in rocks that were 225 million years old, which made it the oldest mammal ever found!

When a scientist discovers a new species, they get to name the species. Dr. Lucas chose the name *Adelobasileus cromptoni*. *Adelo* is Latin for "obscure," or hard to find, and *basileus* means "king." The species was hard to find but pointed toward the future, when mammals would be kings of the animal kingdom.

You can see pictures of the fossil and a drawing of what the mammal probably looked like.

KEYWORD PROMPTS

Adelobasileus cromptoni palaeocritti

WHAT ARE SCIENTISTS HOPING TO LEARN?

The field of paleontology has come a long way, but there are always new questions waiting to be answered. One question we all want the answer to is "Why?" Why does the climate change? Why did the dinosaurs go extinct? Why did mammals evolve?

Earth's climate has changed dramatically through time. It's important to understand how and why the climate has changed in the past. This can help us understand how our current climate is changing and how humans might be affecting the climate.

Scientists are also trying to understand how sensitive ecosystems, such as coral reefs, responded to climate change in the past. This helps them to understand the present. The more we know about the causes of extinction, both background and mass extinctions, the better we understand how and why organisms become extinct today.

New species are continually being discovered. Many of them surprise us with new information. By studying what happened long ago, we can better understand the present and future.

? INVESTIGATE!

It's time to consider and discuss: What questions about fossils do you find most interesting?

SUPPLIES

* newspaper
* bucket for mixing
* sturdy stick for stirring
* 3 cups plaster of Paris
* 2 cups sand
* water
* tempera paint (optional)
* plastic bin the size of a shoebox
* small plastic animals or toys
* 1 cup dirt
* hammer
* chisel
* goggles

FOSSIL DIG

Paleontologists usually have to excavate, or dig out, fossils from different kinds of rock. Create a fossil "dig" of rock layers with fossils, and try your own excavation.

1 Spread out newspaper or work outside. Mix half of the sand and an equal amount of water and plaster in the plastic bucket. Stir until it's the consistency of mud. Add paint if you like.

2 Pour the mixture into the plastic bin and let it settle. Push several plastic animals into the mixture.

3 Mix the dirt and an equal amount of plaster and water in the bucket. Pour it on top of the sand mixture and add more plastic animals.

4 Mix the remaining sand and plaster and an equal amount of water. Pour it on top of the dirt mixture and add more plastic animals.

5 Let the layers harden. Turn the plastic bin over and push out the layers of rock. Put on the goggles and use the hammer and chisel to dig out the animals.

THINGS TO NOTICE: Was the mud or sand mixture easier to dig out? Which kind of rock do you think the sand mixture is most like? Which kind of rock is the dirt mixture most like?

PALEO PUZZLE

Paleontologists don't usually find complete skeletons. See if you can put together your own partial skeleton.

SUPPLIES

* a friend
* 24 popsicle sticks
* 2 markers, 1 black and 1 other color
* clear tape
* shoebox
* enough sand or soil to fill the box
* spoons

1 Each person lays 10 popsicle sticks side by side flat on a table. Tape them together at the top and bottom. Turn them over so the tape is on the back.

2 Using the black marker, draw a picture of a dinosaur on the front so that each popsicle stick has a small part of the picture. Remove the tape and jumble your sticks. Then practice putting your sticks back together to form the picture.

3 Exchange popsicle sticks. Without showing each other, remove two sticks and replace with blank sticks. Fill the shoebox with the soil, then bury all of the sticks in the soil.

4 Carefully dig your soil using the spoons. Once you have dug out all the sticks, put them together. You'll have some gaps in the drawing from the blank sticks. Using the different color marker, draw in the missing pieces.

THINGS TO NOTICE:

Was it harder to put the pieces together after you removed two sticks? Paleontologists rarely find complete skeletons. They must use their knowledge to put together the pieces found.

COOKIE DIG

Paleontologists dig fossils using many different kinds of tools. Try digging out your own yummy fossils!

1 Dig out the chocolate chips and raisins from your cookies. On each type of cookie, use each type of tool—a toothpick, the fork, and the table knife. Set the chips and raisins aside on a plate.

2 Carefully clean the chips and raisins with the tools, your fingernails, and paper towels.

THINGS TO NOTICE: Which cookies were easier to dig out with a toothpick? With a fork or knife? Were you able to get the chips and raisins completely clean? Paleontologists use a variety of different tools to dig out fossils. It depends on the size and type of fossil, as well as the rock it is found in.

SUPPLIES

* chocolate chip cookies, both soft and crisp
* oatmeal raisin cookies
* toothpicks
* fork
* table knife
* plate
* paper towels

INVESTIGATING MORE

Remember the discovery of *Adelobasileus,* the oldest known mammal? Scientists want to know what kind of inner ear bones *Adelobasileus* has. Reptiles have a straight inner ear tube, but mammals have a spiral-shaped inner ear tube. The spiral shape and tiny hairs give mammals much better hearing, which they needed to survive when dinosaurs ruled. *Adelobasileus* was the size of a mouse, and probably hunted insects in trees at night.

Glossary

amber: hard, fossilized resin. Resin is a sticky substance that oozes from trees.

amphibian: a vertebrate animal, such as a frog or salamander, that needs sunlight to keep warm and shade to stay cool. It lays its eggs in water.

archaeology: the study of ancient people through the objects they left behind. A scientist who studies archaeology is a archaeologist.

arthropod: an invertebrate animal with a skeleton on the outside of its body. It has a segmented body and jointed legs. Insects and spiders are arthropods.

atmosphere: the blanket of air surrounding the earth.

atom: a small particle of matter. Atoms are the extremely tiny building blocks of everything.

background extinction: the constant low-level rate of extinction.

biology: the study of living things.

camouflage: the colors or patterns that allow a plant or animal to blend in with its environment.

carbon: an element found in living things, including plants. Carbon is also found in diamonds, charcoal, and graphite.

carbonization: the conversion of organic matter into a carbon film.

carnivore: an animal that eats meat.

carnivorous: feeding on insects or other animals.

chloroplasts: tiny structures in the cell of a green plant where photosynthesis takes place.

climate: the average weather patterns in an area over a long period of time.

climate change: changes to the average weather patterns in an area during a long period of time.

cold-blooded: animals such as snakes that have a body temperature that varies with the surrounding temperature.

correlate: to relate rocks and fossils from one area with another area. Correlation is often used to determine the age of rocks and fossils.

cyanobacteria: microbes that are blue-green in color and use photosynthesis.

decay: to rot.

dromaeosaur: the name for dinosaur raptors. Raptors were small- to medium-sized meat-eaters that walked on two legs with long, grasping fingers and a huge claw on each foot.

ecosystem: a community of organisms that interact with each other and their environment.

environment: everything in nature, living and nonliving, including plants, animals, soil, rocks, and water.

erosion: the gradual wearing away of rock or soil by water and wind.

evaporation: when a liquid heats up and changes to a gas.

evolve: to change over time, sometimes into something more complex.

extinction: the disappearance of a species from the earth.

fossil: the remains of any organism, including animals and plants, that have been preserved in rock.

genus: a group of organisms that consists of one or more species.

geologic timescale: the way the 4.6-billion-year history of the earth is divided up.

geology: the study of the earth and its rocks. A scientist who studies geology is a geologist.

groundwater: water contained underground in the spaces in soil and sediment.

herbivore: an animal that eats plants.

herd: a large group of animals.

igneous rock: rock that forms from cooling magma. Magma is melted rock below the surface of the earth.

index fossil: a type of fossil that is used to identify geologic periods. It correlates rocks from one area with another.

invertebrate: an animal without a backbone.

law of superposition: the scientific law that sedimentary layers are deposited with the oldest on the bottom and the youngest on top.

living fossils: a living species that has changed little from long ago and doesn't have close relatives still alive.

mammal: a type of animal, such as a human, dog, or cat. Mammals are usually born live, feed milk to their young, and usually have hair or fur covering most of their skin.

mass extinction: periods in the earth's history when very large numbers of species die out in a short period of time.

meteorite: a meteor that is not burned up by the earth's atmosphere and hits the earth's surface.

microbe: another word for microorganism.

microorganism: an organism that is so small it can only be seen with a microscope.

Middle Ages: the name for a period of time from around the year 350 to 1450.

minerals: solids that are found in rocks and in the ground. Rocks are made of minerals. Gold and diamonds are precious minerals.

numerical age: the age of a rock or fossil, usually in millions of years.

nutrients: substances in food and soil that living things need to live and grow.

organic: something that is or was living, such as animals, wood, grass, and insects.

organism: any living thing.

ornithischians: dinosaurs that had a hip structure like birds, where the pubic bone points down and backward. All plant-eaters that are not sauropods are ornithischians.

paleontology: the study of the fossils of plants and animals. A scientist who studies paleontology is a paleontologist.

peat: a brown, soil-like material that contains partially decayed plant matter.

petrified wood: a fossil of wood that has been turned to stone.

petrify: to change into stone.

photosynthesis: the process by which green plants and some microorganisms use sunlight, water, and carbon dioxide to make sugars that they use for food.

plankton: microscopic organisms drifting in bodies of water.

predator: an animal that hunts other animals for food.

prey: an animal hunted by a predator for food.

primates: mammals that have large brains, nails on the hands and feet, and a short snout. Apes, monkeys, chimpanzees, and humans are primates.

pterosaur: an extinct flying reptile with featherless wings of the Mesozoic Period.

radioactive decay: the breakdown of an atom into another kind of atom.

radiocarbon dating: a type of radiometric dating that applies to material that was once living. It can only be used for materials that are about 40,000 years old or younger.

radiometric dating: a method to determine the numerical age of a rock or fossil. It uses known rates of radioactive decay.

relative age: the age of a rock or fossil relative to other rocks or fossils.

reptile: an animal usually covered with scales that lays eggs in dry places. Reptiles include snakes, lizards, turtles, and now-extinct dinosaurs.

saurischians: dinosaurs that had a hip structure like lizards, where the pubic bone points forward. All theropods and sauropods are saurischians.

sauropods: a group of plant-eating dinosaurs that walked on four legs and had a long neck and tail.

sedimentary rocks: rocks formed from sediments or the remains of plants or animals. Sedimentary rock can also form from the evaporation of seawater.

sediments: small particles of rocks or minerals, such as clay, sand, or pebbles.

species: a group of living things that are closely related and can produce young.

stromatolite: a rocky mass made of sediments trapped by mats of bacteria.

theory of evolution: a scientific theory that explains how species change over time.

theropods: a group of dinosaurs that walked on two hind legs and included all meat-eaters.

toxic: something that is poisonous.

trackway: a pathway of continuous dinosaur footprints.

tsunami: a long, high sea wave caused by an earthquake or other disturbance.

vertebrate: an animal with a backbone.

warm-blooded: animals such as humans that don't depend on the temperature around them to stay warm.

METRIC CONVERSIONS

Use this chart to find the metric equivalents to the English measurements in this book. If you need to know a half measurement, divide by two. If you need to know twice the measurement, multiply by two. How do you find a quarter measurement? How do you find three times the measurement?

English	Metric
1 inch	2.5 centimeters
1 foot	30.5 centimeters
1 yard	0.9 meter
1 mile	1.6 kilometers
1 pound	0.5 kilogram
1 teaspoon	5 milliliters
1 tablespoon	15 milliliters
1 cup	237 milliliters

BOOKS

Abramson, Andra Serlin, Jason Brougham, and Carl Mehling, *Inside Dinosaurs*. New York: Sterling Publishing, 2010 (fold-out pages, with American Museum of Natural History).

Bonner, Hannah, *When Fish Got Feet, Sharks Got Teeth, and Bugs Began to Swarm: A Cartoon Prehistory of Life Long Before Dinosaurs*. Washington, D.C.: National Geographic, 2007.

Bonner, Hannah, *When Bugs Were Big, Plants Were Strange, and Tetrapods Stalked the Earth: A Cartoon Prehistory of Life Before Dinosaurs*. Washington, D.C.: National Geographic, 2004.

Lambert, David, *Eyewitness Dinosaur*. New York: DK Publishing, 2014.

Larson, Peter, and Kristin Donnan, *Bones Rock! Everything You Need to Know to Be a Paleontologist*. Montpelier, Vermont: Invisible Cities Press, 2004.

Pim, Keiron, *Dinosaurs - The Grand Tour: Everything Worth Knowing About Dinosaurs from Aardonyx to Zuniceratops*. New York: The Experiment, 2014.

Taylor, Paul D., and Aaron O'Dea, *A History of Life in 100 Fossils*. Washington D.C.: Smithsonian Books, 2014.

Thimmesh, Catherine, *Scaly Spotted Feathered Frilled*. New York: Houghton Mifflin Harcourt, 2013.

Woodward, John, *Smithsonian Dinosaur!* New York: DK Publishing, 2014.

Resources

WEBSITES

University of California Museum of Paleontology: *evolution.berkeley.edu*

American Museum of Natural History: *amnh.org/explore/ology/paleontology*

Paleontology activities, games, and information: *fossilsforkids.com*

BBC: *bbc.co.uk/nature/history_of_the_earth*

Fossil Parks and Clubs: *myfossil.org/fossil-parks*

Fossils in National Parks: *paleoportal.org/nps*

QR CODE GLOSSARY

Page 6: *nature.nps.gov/geology/nationalfossilday/index.cfm*

Page 8: *merriam-webster.com*

Page 15: *en.wikipedia.org/wiki/Georges_Cuvier#/media/File:Cuvier_elephant_jaw.jpg*

Page 31: *earthsky.org/earth/shark-attack-preserved-in-fossil-whale-bone*

Page 33: *indiana.edu/~geol105b/images/gaia_chapter_10/stromatolites.htm*

Page 36: *popsci.com/here-science-first-fossil-carnivorous-plant-trap*

Page 50: *history.com/news/discovery-of-oldest-human-fossil-fills-evolutionary-gap*

Page 56: *listofwonders.com/visit-dinosaur-ridge-to-see-the-dinosaur-freeway*

Page 67: *darwinproject.ac.uk/letter/entry-3905*

Page 74: *endangered.org/10-easy-things-you-can-do-to-save-endangered-species*

Page 81: *palaeocritti.com/by-group/mammaliaformes/adelobasileus*

ESSENTIAL QUESTIONS

Introduction: Why do we use geologic time when we talk about the history of the earth? Why not use human time?

Chapter 1: What can fossils tell us about the kinds of environments that existed long ago?

Chapter 2: Why is it important to study both the fossil and the area around the fossil for clues?

Chapter 3: What are some of the different ways humans depend on plants?

Chapter 4: How has the earth's environment influenced how animals have evolved?

Chapter 5: How did the bodies of plant-eating dinosaurs help them survive?

Chapter 6: Why did meat-eating dinosaurs come in such a variety of sizes and abilities?

Chapter 7: When one species evolves or becomes extinct, how does that affect other species?

Chapter 8: What questions about fossils do you find most interesting?

Index

Index